I have known Charlie and Jill for over 30 years. Their songs, teaching, and friendship have always been an encouragement and inspiration. The years following the death of their son took them on a journey through grief none of us would want to take. But unfortunately, so many of us do. Without a proper theology for dealing with sorrow, we can turn to an unhealthy way of dealing with pain. Learning to lament and find peace is a critical part of the process.

Through sharing their experiences and authentic faith, Charlie and Jill offer hope and wisdom to those who are grieving or those near someone dealing with loss.

—Sean Yost
Lead pastor, Redeemer Church
Ponte Vedra, Florida

Fellow travelers. Those were the two words that came to mind as I began reading Charlie and Jill's book—their story. When certain events happen in life, we may feel like we are walking alone, but if you are dealing with an overwhelming sense of loss and grief, it is good to know that someone has walked where you are walking and has journeyed a path similar to yours. If you are looking for a superficial, sugar-coated, sanitized book with cute clichés about death and grief, this is not the book you want to read. However, if you are looking for someone to peel off the veneer and share the reality of their pain from the depths of their hearts, this is a book you will relate to and benefit from. You are not just going to hear about the loss, but also the comfort. Not just the despair, but also the hope. Most importantly, Charlie and Jill point you to the One who is always beside you, to the friend who really does stick closer than a brother, to the One who will never leave nor forsake you.

—Tony Cooke
Bible Teacher and Author

Grief for me, especially after the death of my daughter Megin in 2018, was completely devastating. It was as though I was dropped in a field with no path to follow.

Eventually a small path would slowly appear which I chose to follow, then that almost undetectable path became a trail which slowly turned into a small road, which in time became more and more easy to follow.

Grief is something you never get over—it's at best something you get through.

Charlie and Jill's book can serve as a wonderful tool to help navigate you on your slowly evolving path.

—Matthew Ward
Second Chapter of Acts

We have all been there. A family member, a friend, a co-worker or neighbor loses someone and we do not know what to say. This is a gripping book written from the hearts of Charlie and Jill as they have traveled the road of losing a child. They write with raw honesty and transparency about what they felt (and still do) throughout what has to be life's most tragic journey. Their honesty will help everyone to understand with simple clarity what we can say and should not say to those experiencing the loss of a loved one. They also give hope to people currently going through a loss, that at some point they can move forward with their own lives.

—Pat Bradley
Author, *Born for Rescue*
Crisis Aid International
www.crisisaid.org

We've known Charlie and Jill for decades. We adore them. They've touched our lives and thousands of others with melodies that open Heaven and words to sing that enrich our faith. Now they've written a book to tell you about their dear son Beau, taken from them in an untimely death, and about their impossible journey into the *shalom* of God.

This book is for you, your family, your friends who are in the dark shadow of death. This book is for my wife Marilyn and me and our family. We all lost Jill—our daughter-in-law, our sister-in law—to brain cancer. Forty-one months of suffering—suffering with aftershocks. Our son lost the love of his life a month short of their 25th anniversary. Our three grandchildren? No more mom in this life.

Every Christian knows this verse: "I can do everything through Him, Jesus, who strengthens me." No one seems to know the next verse: "Yet it was good of you to share in my troubles." Somehow, we all manage to live forward, but not without love and encouragement and insight and wisdom from books like this, given to us by godly people like Charlie and Jill who want you to experience fully the life-giving presence of God that shines into the suffocating darkness of Beau's death.

—Dr. Gary D. Kinnaman
Pastor and author

Charlie and Jill LeBlanc are persevering people. By that, I mean they have been through life experiences that have been fun and thrilling and through hardships that broke their hearts. Yet they found that God is near the brokenhearted and saves those who are crushed in spirit.

Their story communicates the ultimate victory that Jesus supplies.

I was with them when their son Beau died. They supported him, poured love into him, and surrounded him with songs of praise. I pray that the reading of this book will create a positive turning point in your life and healing of your heart.

—Pastor Jeff Perry

To live life after the loss of a child is something I can't even understand. Having two daughters myself, I find it hard to comprehend how anyone could move on from that experience, let alone continue doing the everyday things required of them. But not only have Charlie and Jill LeBlanc learned how to move forward and continue their lives in spite of the pain, by writing this book they've found a way to help others who've been through similar experiences. This is what true ministry is all about—to take pain and use it to help others. That's what *When Loss Comes Close to Home* does—it will help to make those painful moments bearable, and ultimately helpful to the world.

I am so incredibly proud to call them not just friends, but family.

—Butch Hartman
Creator, *The Fairly OddParents*

The depth and transparency of Charlie and Jill's experience in losing a loved one is so refreshing! Finally, an honest guide to help all of us to stop covering over or ignoring our losses, while empowering us to feel our grief without shame.

As we lean in to a loving God who wants to heal us and make our lives whole, we find a life of abundance again. Everyone should read this book, because all of us will experience the loss of someone we love, and will need a step-by-step guide to navigate it with honesty and hope.

—Carla Riehl
Christian singer/songwriter
Chicken Soup for the Soul contributor

Charlie and Jill LeBlanc are a deep, deep well of love and compassion. The hard-earned spiritual maturity they developed through this tragic loss of their son is immeasurable. During my husband Reed Grafke's two-year battle with cancer, Charlie and Jill ministered to us as no one else could. They were literally the hands and feet of Jesus in our life day after day and night after night. This book will be a treasure to all who read it. I wholeheartedly recommend it!

—Teri Secrest
Bestselling author

When Loss Comes Close to Home

Harrison House

Shippensburg, PA

The Yarrow flower illustrated on the front cover has long been recognized as a symbol of healing and love. We pray, as you read this, that God's love and healing will saturate your soul.

When Loss Comes Close to Home

FINDING HOPE TO CARRY ON WHEN
DEATH TURNS YOUR WORLD UPSIDE DOWN

Charlie & Jill LeBlanc

In loving memory

of our dear son and brother,

Beau Charles LeBlanc

May 14, 1985–January 14, 2009

You are forever in our hearts.

During the journey of working hard to see our son recover, he designed this image, a musical treble and bass clef mixed with his initial, B. The intention was for all of our family and close friends to receive a celebration tattoo of this after he was cancer-free.

Sadly though, after his passing it became a memorial tattoo which several have taken on in various forms, as a symbol of their love for him.

Dedication

Once you experience loss on a deep level in your family, it makes the ones you still have with you even more cherished. Therefore, we dedicate this book to our beyond-precious daughters,

Camille LeBlanc-Fowler

Cherrie LeBlanc Dye

along with our four beautiful grandsons,

Kingston BeauCharles Fowler

Charles LeBlanc Fowler

Jayce Kimbrough Dye

John Perrey Dye

By the grace of God, we are surviving this nightmare, awaiting the day we get to embrace our dear son and brother again in Heaven, something like this (but *much* more glorious)!

CONTENTS

FOREWORD

My husband, Dave, and I have known Charlie and Jill for over forty years. We've been blessed by their friendship as well as their partnership in ministry, when they led worship at many of our conferences. We've known them in good times and hard times and have seen them live out their faith in Christ when it was easy and when it wasn't. Their commitment and diligence to seek God has been tested many times, and each time, He has helped them grow stronger in their determination to keep going in the most disappointing and painful events in their life.

When Charlie and Jill's son, Beau, passed away after his shocking and traumatic battle with cancer, we were devastated with them and for them. The loss of a child is something I've never had to face, and I can only imagine the overwhelming grief it has caused them—mentally, emotionally, spiritually and even physically. And yet, in the face of this tragedy, even though it caused them to question God, they never abandoned their faith in Him. Knowing them the way we do, this is no surprise.

The journey that's led them to write this book has impacted every single part of their being, and the wisdom and insight they've gained by walking through this experience is invaluable. It took great courage on their part to be transparent about their thoughts and emotions in the days following Beau's death, and it inspires me. I believe their vulnerability is what makes this message so relatable and even hopeful for those who read it.

If you've lost someone dear to you, Charlie and Jill's story will comfort and encourage you to go through your grieving process the way you need to do it...one step at a time. If you want to be a better comforter and encourager to others who are grieving, their story will help you understand how to do that too.

Charlie and Jill know what it means to really live for Jesus, and their passion is to help as many people as they can to personally experience the life Jesus died for them to have. I'm confident that you'll discover help in your time of loss and grief in the pages of this book.

—Joyce Meyer, Bible Teacher and Best-selling Author

FOREWORD

Everyone suffers loss, some more than others. Jesus said we would suffer tribulation (John 16:33). It's part of living in a fallen world. So, it's not a matter of if, it's a matter of when, and how we deal with it.

Charlie and Jill suffered the loss of a beloved son prematurely. I got to witness their journey through that time up close and personal. And although each one of us navigates life's hardships differently, I've seen them persevere and arrive at a good place where they are not only receiving healing, but are willing and able to help others through the process.

Anyone who has been down the same road you are traveling has information that can help you. They could tell you of the weather conditions or closures or places to stop and see along the way. Likewise, Charlie and Jill have experienced what you are going through, and they have valuable information that could make a huge difference in your journey.

The Lord loves you and is with you every step of the way, regardless of what it looks or feels like. He is Faithful, and the LeBlancs will inspire you with the lessons they have learned through life's hardest blows. There is joy and hope if you press through to the end. Charlie and Jill will help you along the way.

—Andrew Wommack

PREFACE

For years, when we mentioned to others that we are writing a book about our grief journey, the overwhelming response has been, "Please do it and ASAP!"

Since the beginning, life has thrown some awful curves to many dear people all around the world. Even Genesis chapter 3 in the Bible shows us the ultimate failure of God's first family and the ensuing pain, not only for Adam and Eve but for all of mankind. Then in chapter 4 they experienced the ultimate heartache—one of their boys being murdered by his brother. Can you even imagine that?

There are so many devastating stories of loss, horrific tragedies, and agonizing sorrow throughout history. In our case, it was the death of our son. The pain was almost unbearable. Even knowing he went straight into the arms of Jesus to suffer no more, we were left in the wake of heartbreak and grief we had no idea existed. Prior to this, I would hear people talk about unthinkable hardship in their lives, and I just couldn't comprehend what it would be like...until this.

Up to that time, life in general for us had been pretty good, so much that Jill was literally about to purchase the ever-so-popular "Life Is Good" T-shirt, hat, and bumper sticker, since this was basically our experience. With us both growing up in (fairly) functional middle-class Christian homes, we met Jesus in our teens, married, gave birth to three little ones, followed "the call" after Bible college, and began traveling in ministry. We wrote and recorded our music, preached and sang in countless churches across the nations, and led worship in conferences for many great Bible teachers. We loved God with all our hearts, and we were very grateful for salvation and Heaven, but we had not experienced tragedy like some had. We didn't understand this kind of pain, resulting in the passion some displayed who had been through hell and seen God pull them through with His loving, gracious arms.

Now we get it.

We are also now more passionate about God and His Word, and amazed at His mercy and grace, which pulled us through the worst nightmare we could have ever imagined—the loss of our own son. We watched him die before our very eyes while we prayed, believed, worshiped, rebuked, bound, and spoke faith and life to his body, but nothing changed! The confusion, anger, disappointment, pain, and sorrow were indescribable.

It is very hard to explain grief on this level, but we will do our best in this book. We will try to share what it's like to have this kind of tragedy disrupt normal life, and more importantly, how we survived.

If you have lost something or someone precious in your life, our desire is to encourage you and give birth to hope that you will get to the other side of it and be able to breathe again, and even at some point, dream again. And even more, to be able to trust and believe again.

These are all things that took time for us; however, through God's love, mercy, grace and patience, we have landed in a good place—not an easy place, but a place of leaning on and resting in His help and grace every day.

Even as we write this book, we are challenged with troubling memories, and our hearts have broken many times while endeavoring to share the journey. But we pray our story may help you and possibly bring light to your path if you are walking in the darkness of a tragedy, be it the loss of a loved one, a marriage, career, investment, a dream, or anything you valued.

No matter what has come your way, just know there is a way through. Even though we don't have all the answers, we will do our best to share with you what helped us and what didn't, with our deepest desire being that you will be strengthened in your journey of recovery.

In hope,
Charlie and Jill

You never leave me, You never forsake me.

Though my world turns upside down,

Your peace can still be found.

You live inside me, Your presence to guide me.

No matter what I'm going through I'm

gonna keep my eyes on You!

—"You Never Leave Me" by Charlie LeBlanc,
from the album *Your Love Remains*[1]

INTRODUCTION

This book is a story of great love.

And great faith.

A great battle and a devastating defeat.

Great sorrow, great despair, being reconciled to a great God, and now better equipped to help others.

On January 14, 2009, our world turned upside down after losing our twenty-three-year-old son to aggressive, metastatic thyroid cancer. To say the least, it's been a tough road. Beau was our only son and an amazing young man. He was very talented, full of charisma, extremely funny and a joy to be around. His absence left a gaping, larger-than-life hole in our family and in our hearts, and for some time we weren't sure we would survive the magnitude of this loss in our lives.

Several years and innumerable outpourings-of-God's-love later, we have survived. And we now know it is our calling to help others walking this journey, endeavoring to bring comfort and encouragement the way the Lord has so gently and faithfully helped us.

This book begins with us sharing our story of the loss that so majorly affected us, along with our daughters and many others whose lives were touched by our precious boy and crushed by his death. As the story continues, we carry on sharing many of the life lessons learned in the process.

At times the writing is very raw and candid, not hiding our thoughts and feelings in order to spare offense. We aren't looking for anyone's pity or attention, but want to relate a gut-level picture of what we (and so many) have sustained.

Our extreme desire is to impart hope and lift the souls of the broken through what we've experienced, as well as give those walking alongside a glimpse of what it's like in these tragic situations, further preparing you to be a blessing to the hurting, like Jesus was when He walked on Earth.

Through these chapters, we pray you will find hope to carry on in life, knowing God will bring you along day by day, minute by minute, one step at a time.

May God help us all to be better examples of "Jesus with skin on."

QUICK START GUIDE FOR THE BEREAVED AND THEIR SUPPORTERS

We are so sorry for your tragic loss. Our hearts break for the pain you are suffering. As you read, we are praying for you to find solace, affirmation, and hope, so you as well can survive your worst nightmare.

So, how *do* you survive when your child dies?

Or your brother?

Or sister?

Or spouse?

Or close parent, family, or friend?

Psalm 34:18 says, *"The Lord is close to the brokenhearted; He rescues those whose spirits are crushed"* (NLT). He is right there with you. All the time. You do not have to walk this journey alone, and please know He will carry you when you feel you can't carry on.

Bereaved, adjective

—suffering the death of a loved one. "The grief of the bereaved parents seemed to be without limit."[2]

How appropriate is this definition!

As one who is bereaved, please:

~ Let yourself cry. You must allow this, or it will come back at a time when you *really* don't expect it, want it, or can afford it.

~ Take only one hour or one moment at a time. Don't think too far ahead—for now, only focus on today.

~ Surround yourself with "safe friends"—those you trust and can be at ease with.

~ Be careful who you share your deepest grief with. As much as you love certain people, not everyone will be able to understand.

TO THOSE WALKING BESIDE

And what do you do when your close friend or relative experiences loss?

Unless you've been there yourself, it's really hard to grasp the depths of what your friend or loved one is living in—walking though the unthinkable.

In these chapters, we hope to unlock some secrets to what helps and what doesn't, and for becoming a safe place for your special person to find solace.

A few starter tips:

~ Just be there—don't avoid the situation because it's uncomfortable.

~ Let your actions show how much you care.

~ Let them freely vent or grieve without fear of judgment.

~ Don't try to "fix them"—just love them.

~ Let yourself "go there"—weep with those who weep.

*All praises belong to the God and Father
of our Lord Jesus Christ. For He is the **Father of
tender mercy** and the **God of endless comfort.**
He **always** comes alongside to comfort us in every
suffering so that we can come alongside those who
are in any painful trial. We can bring them this
same comfort that God has poured out upon us.*

—2 Corinthians 1:3–4 TPT

PART 1

In this first section, we will be sharing with you our own story of tragic, and what seemed like sudden loss, how we eventually began to resurface after almost drowning in our sorrows, and insights we gained along the way. We share much affirmation and encouragement to those walking this road, and pray you receive hope for your own recovery.

CHAPTER ONE

In the Beginning

"Hey, Madre..."

After he moved to Phoenix from St. Louis at nineteen, this became Beau's standard greeting when he would call his momma.

Our phone conversation that day in early 2008 was one of light catching up, with an "Oh, by the way, I just got fired from my job," quickly thrown in there!

After our discussion of everything that went down (nothing jail-worthy—he served at a restaurant and was caught one-too-many times dipping into the mashed potatoes in the kitchen!), things switched gears.

"Hey, Mom, my throat's been sore for a while now..."

I could tell by the shift in his tone that it was concerning him.

In the spring of 2008, our beautiful twenty-two-year-old son was diagnosed with inoperable, stage-four, metastatic thyroid cancer, spread throughout his entire neck region.

From the time of diagnosis, it was a nine-month, white-knuckle roller-coaster ride of devastating news, then good news, and then more bad news, up then down again, all the while trusting God for a tremendous outcome. We were standing on God's promises and praying, studying, and doing everything spiritually and humanly possible to help our son survive this onslaught against his life and ours as a family.

But fast-forward to January 2009, the day when our hearts were ripped out of our chests and we said our tearful and broken goodbyes to our son. Here's how it played out.

It was the wee hours of January 14.

"Okay, y'all! Let me know if you need anything. Goodnight!" I kissed Beau on the forehead, told him I loved him, then started upstairs. It would be the first time both Charlie and I had gotten to sleep in our bed at the same time in quite a while, now that both our daughters and Beau's closest cousins and friends were there to look after him.

The last two days, our home had been beautifully and amazingly flooded with friends and family, praying, worshiping, and standing with us for this miracle which we believed so firmly in our hearts we would soon see with our eyes! It *seemed* that we were out of time "in the natural," and the "supernatural" would kick in very shortly.

1:00 a.m. As we got in bed and my head hit the pillow, I recall being able to rest and then sleep. Little did I realize what was about to transpire.

2:00 a.m. Cami came up to our room, opened the door and said, "Mom and Dad, Beau is throwing up."

Throwing up was something we'd dealt with *a lot* the previous nine months, not always being able to tell how well he was digesting the liquid food from his enteral feeding device with a tube directly into his stomach. My first thought was, *Dang! Why did I keep the feeding machine going?!* We'd had it on most of the evening.

We sprang out of bed a bit disoriented and hurried downstairs to find him in the recliner, unresponsive.

He wasn't breathing. There was a nervous tension in the air.

We quickly moved him onto the floor so I could give him CPR, which was unsuccessful.

I can still hear the roar of his sisters, his cousins, and closest friends, shouting his name at the top of their voices as he first slipped away, in hopes of jolting him back to consciousness.

"Beau!! *Beau!!* BEAU!!!!" But there his body lay, unresponsive to our desperate efforts to bring him back.

As our noble attempts became feeble, which then became failed attempts to revive and keep him with us, all the shouts turned into prayers. Charlie then tenderly embraced him as only a loving father could, and began to call Beau back from the Other Side, command his body to be healed, and Beau's spirit to come back into his lifeless frame.

We all greatly anticipated and expected that any moment Beau's eyes would open, he'd begin breathing, and rejoin us all who loved him so dearly.

As prayers continued, we also worshiped as our son-in-law beautifully played the piano, trusting the Lord with the safe return of our son, brother, nephew, cousin, and friend, knowing the Lord was our only hope for Beau's resurrection.

We called two close minister friends, requesting their ongoing prayers for our miracle to manifest.

The minutes became hours, yet we continued worshiping in joyful expectation of seeing him wake up at any moment. Little by little our family room became less and less occupied, and eventually the only ones left in the room were Beau's sisters, brother-in-law, his aunt and cousin, Beau's father, me, and our pastor, who'd come over around 4:00 a.m.

As Beau's still body lay there after about four hours, my mind began to be battered with thoughts.

It was like so many action films where the main characters are fighting a fierce battle against a raging enemy. As they become outnumbered and fighting their hardest, they give what would be their last push of strength, hope, and courage.

So it seemed with my heart.

"Any time now… Come on, Beau… Come on, Lord! Why isn't this happening? I can't believe he hasn't come back yet… Is all this that we believe true or not? You would think, if it *is* true, we would have our miracle by now…Your will be done, Lord, and I *know* Your will is for Beau to live." I tried my best to escape that twilight zone as I desperately clung onto the faith to continue believing and trusting in God's faithfulness, despite the constant bombardment now raging inside.

In some movies, while the battle rages on, we watch in slow motion as our heroes are taken down one by one until none are left standing. In the same way, just as the light succumbs to darkness at the end of each day, my emotions slowly began turning from hope, peace, trust and joyful expectation into bewilderment, frustration and questioning.

Our son was not getting up, much less even waking up. His battle-weary body laid there lifeless. Breathless. Where was the miracle? How long should we continue? If it were a matter of time, I would have kept going. We all would have. With joyful expectation, even. I wouldn't have cared if it took all day, regardless of missing a night's sleep. Who cares about losing some sleep when your child's life is in the balance? We would carry on praying and believing and commanding if it meant he would come back to us in a healed body!

But where do you stop? How do you know when it's over— when he's not coming back? You hear the stories of prayer vigils continuing for days over a dead body. Is *that* what we should do? We would. If…

It was 7:00 a.m. I looked around. Cherrie was sitting curled up on the floor near Beau, meditating on scriptures she had gathered. Cami was kneeling at Beau's side praying and singing. I had taken shifts with my son-in-law and niece on the piano playing soft, worshipful music as we continued seeking the Lord. But the last hour I was on the floor leaning against one of the blow-up mattresses that we'd all taken turns sleeping on the last few weeks. I was fighting the battle of a lifetime in my mind, and was beginning to feel the sun setting on my hope and my faith.

The room became quiet. It had been five hours since Beau crossed over. Charlie, sitting on the hearth of the fireplace where a few smoldering embers were still barely flickering, not unlike our hearts, looked at our pastor and said, "What should we do?"

As a wise man who had faced this situation too many times, he answered, "If you want to keep on praying, so will I! I'm here to fully support you guys."

All eyes were now on Charlie. He looked at me and back at Pastor Jeff.

"I guess we should let him go."

"No! NO!! *NOOOOOOO!!!*" The mourning that began to flood the room from the deepest places of our broken hearts, I will never forget.

Cami, who was there beside him, was now kneeling over his body, her hands on his face, wailing and calling his name, "Nooooo! NOOOOOO!! Beau, you can't leave us!!"

Cherrie's face was buried in her hands, sobbing, her soul crushed.

Charlie was quietly fighting back his own sobs as he watched his daughters so painfully mourn the loss of their beloved brother, wondering how this could possibly be.

My sister and niece slipped out of the room to give us space.

Me? I was sitting against the mattress, dumbfounded. Speechless. Internalizing.

What just happened? Where did we go wrong? Why did Beau not come back to us? What about all the healing scriptures? The visions? On and on the questions flooded my soul.

Yes, there were tears in my eyes as our hearts were all breaking into pieces, but I couldn't cry. I was too upset to cry. Bewilderment had given way to anger. I was becoming furious. In my heart I vented, *What is up with this, God?! Are you the Almighty One or not?! I've been crying out to You to show us where we've missed the disconnect between the spirit and the natural as he declined. You could've shown us if we were praying wrong. We have consistently prayed and trusted You for wisdom and direction, standing on **Your promises**, and believed we were following Your lead. What the heck happened?!!!"*

Trust was broken.

Honestly, some may not understand this, but it was like a sudden death—the thought that Beau would die was the *furthest* thing from our minds.

I was so furious that I could hardly speak.

All the prophesies, the dreams, the visions—all gone.

What we couldn't see with our eyes (but knew in our hearts) was, he blasted off out of his emaciated Earth-suit into an indescribable, wonderful, and glorious new body and home, where we will reunite one day and be together for eternity. We can hardly imagine the joy of that reunion!

But it was the furthest thought from all of us at that moment in time.

Needless to say, our lives changed forever that day.

We watched our son slip away like trying to hold water in our hands, and then die in our home. We saw his suffering—his fighting for every breath as the cancer had eventually filled both lungs. Once you see something, you can never "unsee" it, and we battled with recurring flashbacks for many, *many* months afterward.

We were *so broken*, and weren't sure at the time if we would *ever* recover.

I cry out, "My splendor is gone! Everything I had hoped for from the Lord is lost!"—Lamentations 3:18, NLT

CHAPTER TWO

What Just Happened?!

The thought of my suffering ... is bitter beyond words.

—Lamentations 3:19, NLT

As the days passed, I (Jill) found myself so bewildered and disoriented.

I was so used to living in a very close relationship with God—we would fellowship together all day long. Prayer was like breathing to me.

Before.

But now? How do you talk to someone you feel is at least partially responsible for letting your child die?

And before that, suffer?

So I wouldn't.

I caught myself from speaking thoughtless "Christianese" phrases, which habitually and often found their way to the tip of my tongue—a "Praise the Lord" and "Hallelujah" here. "Thank You, Jesus" and "Amen!" there. It was all so automatic before—almost thoughtless. But now?

Proverbs 13:12 in the Good News Translation so poignantly describes the condition of our souls at that time, *"When hope is crushed, the heart is crushed."*

Actually, I didn't speak to the Lord for weeks. Much less "praise" Him. I would honestly stop myself from praying about something, which was my continual M.O. before. It's not that I wanted to walk away from Him, but I was so confused.

So broken.

So disheartened.

I felt so betrayed …

Was I living in denial before? I don't know. It sure didn't seem like it. I felt my faith was genuine, birthed from my spirit and God's Word, but there was a disconnect somewhere. Yes, there certainly was—and a big one.

Or maybe it was a small one.

It only takes a small break in a cord, one broken copper wire to interrupt an electric current from flowing through to an entire house. My disconnect could've been small and seemingly insignificant, but it sure did create a big chasm. And the difficult thing is, how could I move forward when I thought I was believing right?

What now?

In the coming days, which became weeks, as the reality that our baby boy was gone from this life continued setting in more each day, my personal struggle grew deeper. Oh yes, without a doubt, *he* is happy, cancer-free now, breathing deeply, and living, dancing, and running (and probably playing drums) in the Lord's presence! What more could a mother want? Right?!

Of course, I am *so* happy for him! The intense suffering is over. He is free and complete, never again to wrestle with sin or sickness, full of joy and peace that we can only dream about.

The loss is on this side.

He was larger than life to all those who knew him. Uber talented. *So* funny. A joy to our family and all his friends. So creative. So fun to be around. Full of shock value to keep us laughing. A great musician to play with, and such a deep musical connection for his dad. And not to mention, Dad's fashion guide. And always challenging us spiritually, in the best sense of the word.

A. Huge. Loss.

And he physically suffered so much. We watched his body waste away for nine months. We did everything we could physically, spiritually, medically, naturally. But it wasn't enough to keep him here.

So we carry on with only memories now, along with the joy of knowing we will be together again in another realm. "Oh, what a day that will be!"[3]

After three or four weeks of not speaking to the Lord, I began to realize several nice things would happen here and there—a special text, an unexpected financial gift, a comped meal, a lightness in my heart, an especially beautiful sunset. It was uncanny *so many* little things like this seemed to suddenly start happening. Then one day, it's like my eyes were opened and it hit me: *Hmmmm! All this has God's fingerprints on it.*

He was not put off by my questions, my harsh challenges to Him, my silence, my closed heart. On the contrary—I experienced during that time a deep level of His love for me that I could have never imagined.

He knew I was hurting. He knew I was broken. He knew my faith in Him was shattered. He knew I felt betrayed. And He did not scold me, try to teach me not to doubt Him, or correct me.

He. Just. Loved. Me.

Isaiah 42:3 describes the Lord's beautiful heart toward the hurting: *"A bruised reed He will not break, and a dimly burning wick He will not extinguish; He will faithfully bring forth justice"* (NASB).

John 21 shares an interesting nugget. One evening after Jesus was gone and the disciples were dealing with the disillusionment and depression of their seemingly failed mission, Simon announced he was going fishing—hoping to at least get something accomplished. The others joined him, and they fished all night without catching anything. At dawn, Jesus was at the shore and called out, asking if they had caught any. Still a ways from shore, *they didn't recognize him right off.* He then told them to throw out their nets on the other side to find some. Of course they made a haul of fish, then John realized the situation and said to Peter, *"It's the Lord!"* (v. 7). And you *know* they *all* must've thought this whole scenario seemed awful familiar!

> *"Now come and have some breakfast!" Jesus said. None of the disciples dared to ask Him, "Who are you?" They knew it was the Lord.* (John 21:12 NLT)

He let them see His "fingerprints."

Through one random act of kindness after another, Jesus was showing His deep love for me. I didn't perceive Him at first. I just thought, *Well that's cool,* when things happened. But day after day He continued compounding His kindness my way, trying to show me His deep compassion, His tenderness toward my broken soul, and His unceasing mercy to both of us. He was in my boat with me, though I didn't recognize Him at first.

He was working on winning my heart back.

> *The Lord is compassionate and gracious, slow to anger, abounding in love.* (Psalm 103:8 NIV)

Our patient, loving Heavenly Father embraced us both as someone gravely injured in battle. At first, for weeks, He constantly held and carried us. Even though we still had so many questions, felt betrayed, and our faith felt destroyed, He ever-so-tenderly began to let us know His loving arms were holding us and strengthening us.

Like in the parable of the good Samaritan, He poured His oil of comfort and His wine of healing into our wounded souls and took care of us. Then, little by little, as we slowly recovered, He would patiently and graciously help us take baby steps until we could walk securely and eventually trust Him once again. Jesus certainly was (and *is*) our good Samaritan! (Luke 10:30–35)

Eventually, we came to this place:

I will never forget this awful time, as I grieve over my loss.

Yet I still dare to hope when I remember this:

The faithful love of the Lord never ends!

His mercies never cease.

Great is His faithfulness;

His mercies begin afresh each morning.

(Lamentations 3:20–23 NLT)

How precious are Your thoughts of me,

Outnumbering the sands in the sea

I'm humbled by Your infinite ways, forever I will stand amazed

I love You Lord, I love You Lord, I'll worship You forever

I cannot escape the wonders of Your grace

And all Your precious love to me

I cannot escape the wonders of Your grace

And all that You have done for me

I love You Lord, I love You Lord, I'll worship You forever.[4]

—"Worship You Forever" by Jill LeBlanc,
from the album *Your Love Remains*

CHAPTER THREE

The Aftermath

*My flesh and my heart may fail, but God is the strength
of my heart and my portion forever.*

—Psalm 73:26 NIV

What I (Charlie) am about to share is very raw and honest.
It's not pretty, but I tried my best to remember my feelings
and review my journals in an effort to help you, the reader,
comprehend a little bit of how hard it was—not for sympathy,
but for hope that you will be encouraged how God can bring
you through the darkest times in your life. If you haven't
experienced something like this, our hopes are that you can
now be more compassionate with someone who has suffered a
loss, or someone dealing with similar issues.

After Beau died, Jill and I took a sabbatical for about three
months and did nothing but try to breathe, reflect, pray, and

cry. A lot. This was the hardest thing either of us had ever gone through in our thirty years of marriage and our entire lives, and we really weren't sure if either of us could make it—not referring to our marriage as much as just our own lives and our hearts, being able to bear this pain and get through the disappointment.

We felt like we were lost and had lost everything on several fronts. It's one thing to lose a child and bear that pain, but as Spirit-filled, Bible-believing Christians, we also had to reconcile what just took place in light of our faith in God and His Word. How could this have happened, and how could a loving God let this happen?

We graduated from a Jesus-centered, faith-and-healing Bible school, where we were taught and believe that Jesus carried our sins *and* sicknesses, as written in Isaiah 53, and this is normal Christianity! We cut our teeth on scriptures that declared God's love and favor for us, how He would protect us from every evil work, and nothing would harm us, by any means.

Jill and I had been in full-time music and Bible-teaching ministry for most of our married life, and mixed into that we had the privilege of leading worship with two of the greatest Bible teachers on the planet—where we heard *and saw* testimonies of God's deliverance and healings on a regular basis.

Therefore, we looked at this sickness and attack on our son's life, and ours, as an easy thing for God, and we knew we would soon be among those who would tell about His grace and healing in our family. With all we had learned about Jesus' healing atonement on the cross and the authority He gave us, and in particular to me as Beau's father, we had full confidence that "this too shall pass." There were all the prayers and promises of God that we and so many had prayed over Beau all his life, along with all the prophecies that had been spoken over him since an infant concerning his future ministry.

So you can see—our loss was a battle and a problem on several fronts: The painful loss of a child we love, and the painful loss of our faith in a God, which we had a great relationship with for more than thirty years. Something wasn't right here, and we weren't sure how to navigate through this!

To say the least, we were mad, confused, and hurt. We felt betrayed by God and preachers and doctors. Nothing seemed to work out like we had planned, much less how we had been taught and believed it would. It was a complete trainwreck and failure, and it seemed there were no answers to the hardest questions of "how?" and "why?"

Part of me wanted to die—it just hurt so bad! And honestly, for a while I lost my own will to live. With this much pain, confusion, and disappointment, I just didn't want to go on. I thought about ending my own life, but I knew immediately I couldn't do that to my wife and our two daughters whom I love so much. How could I be so selfish to end my pain but multiply theirs?

But to be perfectly honest, part of me did die.

I had thoughts of just trying to drink the pain away under a bridge somewhere for the rest of my life. But once again, I didn't want to inflict any more pain on my family since we were all hurting so much already.

The only remaining option, as difficult as it was: look to God!

Then I remembered the passage of scripture where the disciples were between a rock and a hard place with Jesus. He was saying things they and others didn't understand, and most people decided to leave because His words were just too hard to reconcile. *"Then Jesus said to the twelve, 'Do you also want to go away?' But Simon Peter answered Him, 'Lord, to whom shall we go? You have the words of eternal life'"* (John 6:67–68).

That scripture rang in my ears. I wanted to run, but where?

Psalm 139:7 also spoke to my soul:

Where can I go from Your Spirit?
Or where can I flee from Your presence?

I finally resolved that there really wasn't anywhere I could go but to God, or *at least* try to get into a neutral position—not running to or from the Lord, since I just didn't know how to trust Him anymore. I just wasn't sure if going toward Him would be a safe place. Nevertheless, it was *a place* to be.

I always knew He was a God of love and He wasn't the author of this kind of tragedy, but it was still hard to reconcile everything that had happened.

In my confusion there were a couple of things I did remember: He Comforts those who mourn, and He is the Healer of broken hearts. I needed both of these. Desperately!

Blessed are those who mourn, for they shall be comforted. (Matthew 5:4)

He heals the brokenhearted and binds up their wounds. (Psalm 147:3)

I knew I needed Him to help me in this recovery and help alleviate this pain, even though I was still upset and felt like He didn't seem to help when I needed Him the most!

So it was a hesitant embrace, returning to Jesus, but a necessary one. I decided I would come to Him, start all over, and receive the simple things that I needed, like His love and comfort, and leave the questions for later.

But it wasn't easy—it was a daily battle of:

~ Questioning myself

~ Questioning God, His Word, His love, the integrity of His Word

~ Wondering what went wrong and why it went wrong

~ Wondering why our prayers were not effective

~ Questioning my authority and my prayers, and feeling responsible for this tragedy

~ Condemnation for not being the man of God I felt I should have been, to be able to rescue my son

And here's a big one:

~ Asking, why didn't the Holy Spirit show us how to pray and what the root of the problem was so we could have prayed more effectively? After all, we continually asked for wisdom!

In addition, I was plagued by these thoughts:

~ Was it God's will? *No!*

~ Was it just "Beau's time"? *No!*

~ Was the devil really involved at all? *Yes!*

~ But, how could the enemy get through our prayers? *I just don't know!*

I didn't know or understand it all. And in some ways, I still don't. So as you can see, it was a major battle in my (and Jill's) mind. We had to consistently be *"casting down arguments and every high thing that exalts itself against the knowledge of God, bringing every thought into captivity to the obedience of Christ."* (2 Corinthians 10:5)

After months of mental battles, I had to come to a place of basically believing and receiving what I could from God, and just placing the unanswered questions on the shelf before Him. He would either show me the answers or, if I wasn't ready to receive the answers, it could mean I wouldn't know until I get to Heaven.

Eventually I began to reach out to God in thanksgiving and worship for everything He has done for me, in giving me salvation and eternal life, and yes, for the reality of Heaven. Especially now.

Heaven became sweeter to me than ever before! Of course, when someone you love is in Heaven, you appreciate it way more and you look forward to your Heavenly home. Knowing the Lord has Beau in His arms is now *very* precious to us all!

I just had to live in what I *did* know and not in what I didn't know. What did I know? I knew God was good and I knew Beau was in Heaven with Him. I knew Beau was blessed beyond words and in a much better place, and ultimately, he had received everything we are all so looking forward to! I had to leave the unknowns for another time—like, "Why?" "What if?" "How could this have happened?" "Where was God?"

These questions will drive you mad if you keep thinking about them. So in times like these I had to remember how Paul exhorted us to think on good things: *"And now, dear brothers and sisters, one final thing. Fix your thoughts on what is true, and honorable, and right, and pure, and lovely, and admirable. Think about things that are excellent and worthy of praise."* (Philippians 4:8 NLT)

This wasn't easy, but I had to do my best to think on the positive things or I would have buried myself in an endless nightmare of grief, anger, fear and disappointment. No doubt about it, it was a battle! Even knowing this scripture and so many others deep down inside, it was still hard to put it all in practice. Many times it was hard to sleep, because that's when your mind starts to go where you don't want it to go (your loved one's journey, the moment of their passing, the disappointment, the "What the hell just happened?!" and the reality of never getting to enjoy your dear one on this side of Heaven again). I had to do my best to keep my thoughts reined in.

We were in San Diego taking time off to recover, when one quiet afternoon I reclined back and began nodding off for a nap. As I did, my mind began "going there"—to that dreadful place of despair, like it had been the last few weeks. This time I said in my heart, *No! I'm not going there! Instead I'm going to think about Beau in Heaven.* As difficult as that was, I made my thoughts go to that happier place, then I experienced glorious peace as I drifted into a short but much-needed rest.

Now, let me say again—even though we knew beyond a shadow of doubt Beau was in Heaven, this still wasn't something that helped us at first, especially when someone would "remind us" of it (like we might've forgotten?). In fact, we feel this is one of the weakest words of comfort someone can give when one is hurting. It just doesn't help. At least, it didn't help us (or most others we've talked to). But after time and with the help of the Holy Spirit, we occasionally would "see" Beau in Heaven in our hearts and minds, especially during worship services and spiritual times of prayer and meditation.

Knowing I have family waiting for me there makes Heaven sweeter than ever. Especially since my dad died just three months after Beau, and then my mom passed about two years later, and now Jill's mom and dad have both followed.

We look forward to seeing them all again, and *especially* giving our beautiful son Beau a great big embrace!

*We are **surrounded** by so great a cloud of witnesses.* (Hebrews 12:1)

O to live in the Light of Heaven,

In the light of the radiance of God

It must be magical to look around and all you see is love

Imagine no more darkness, forgetting all the pain

And laughing with our Lord face-to-face

It will be wonderful someday to live in the Light of Heaven.[5]

—"Light of Heaven" by Jill LeBlanc,
from the album *Your Love Remains*

CHAPTER FOUR

Every Journey Is Unique

You keep track of all my sorrows.
You have collected all my tears in your bottle.
You have recorded each one in your book.

—Psalm 56:8 NLT

I (Jill) want to point out that in a subject as vast as surviving loss and the grief journey, we realize we are speaking from our point of view and share generalities we, along with others we've spoken to, have suffered and experienced.

One thing we learned very early on is that everyone grieves differently!

Just as each of us has individual DNA, fingerprints, and irises, *everyone* has their own healing journey. It is *not* one size fits all. Each person's path to recovery is unique. There is no pre-set pattern to follow. For some it is easier than for others. Sometimes the grief experience is linked to the relationship they had with the deceased, and sometimes it's linked to their relationship with God.

But for most, it takes a *long time* to really bounce back from the loss of a close loved one, especially a sudden or untimely death. In his monumental work, *Living When A Loved One Has Died*, Rabbi Earl Grollman writes, "There is no way to predict how you will feel. The reactions of grief are not like recipes, with given ingredients, and certain results. Each person mourns in a different way. Grief is universal. At the same time, it is extremely personal."[6]

When I was growing up, I would hear people talk about "the grieving process," something taught in basic psychology, also referred to as the five stages of grief:

1. denial

2. anger

3. bargaining

4. depression

5. acceptance[7]

There are generalities in all these that can be applied in many situations, but the grief journey really is as unique as the individual experiencing it.

One friend, although shocked, bewildered, and numb, *never* blamed God for the sudden death of her husband. Another deeply devoted Christian friend, upon losing her son suddenly, was also shocked and paralyzed emotionally, but believes the

Lord gave her scriptures referring to why it happened, which helped her cope. Another friend became furious at God at the death of their child and threw out every Christian doctrine they'd ever been taught, at least for a time.

Each one has their own journey to travel—it's their road to walk, and in most cases it's a hard one. We must keep them in prayer as they recover!

There will always be those whose loved one's passing brought relief and a fresh wind into their sails, especially after a long illness, and still those whose situations were unique or unusual and they did not suffer emotional devastation. We were both like this when our parents passed away. As Charlie mentioned, each one of the four left us *after* our son did— Beau was the first extremely close relation either of us had lost. So by the time our parents died, that grief did not come *near* to what we had walked through previously, even though Charlie's father passed barely three months afterward. As "they" say, "A child's death should never precede their own parents'," but ours did. The prior anguish we experienced caused *our* own parents' passings to pale in comparison. We're not saying in any way we didn't love them, and we do miss them, but I think you understand. They all lived full lives and died in their mid-to-late eighties.

Some people, because of their circumstances, are forced back to work too soon afterward because it's not possible to take a proper leave of absence, which would have allowed them to grieve and work through those early days and weeks. Some establishments only provide a *three-day* bereavement leave, and others none at all! If sufficient time or attention is not given to the griever, allowing time to mourn and process, it can be devastating in the long run, really delaying and crippling their healing process.

On the other hand, in the case of empty nesters where one passes away leaving the other to live alone, they can often find help and comfort from their friends at work rather than being left alone in an empty house. Older adults can really battle with loneliness and even fear after spending years with their spouse, then suddenly finding themselves alone and on their own.

Personally, we were extremely blessed to be able to go away for a month to a condo our dear brother and sister-in-law graciously shared with us. I don't know how we would have survived having to go back to work, even though our "work" is ministry. Regardless, being around groups of people was *the last* thing we wanted to do or felt capable of.

There is no timetable to grief. Anyone that tells you that there is, doesn't know your grief. You will be feeling a variety of emotions, sometimes all at once. Feelings of relief, frustration, anger, rage, anxiety, giddiness, and sadness are all normal.[8]

Looking from the outside, we just don't know the pain *so many people* live with on a daily basis, surviving losing a close loved one. Unfortunately for some, they grieve for decades, even until the day they leave this life and are greeted by their Savior and loved one in Heaven.

We pray your grief journey can be healthy, as difficult as it is, until you reach a functional plateau in life and begin to move forward again.

I (Charlie) would like to emphasize, as we addressed above, you and your loved ones will grieve differently! You have to make space for that. What blesses them may not bless you, and vice versa. Try your best to be sensitive to this, to avoid hurting anyone. Walking through grief is *a lot* of work!

In the early days after our loss, I remember Jill loved looking at pictures of Beau and laughing or crying over them. Even though it would stir up emotion, she loved having that connection in her soul with her departed son. Yet for me, when I saw his photos, it hurt so deeply and made me miss him even more.

When people would tell us what a great guy he was (and we got a lot of that!), Jill would *feed* off that because it made her feel closer to him. Yet to me, it would magnify my loss even more, and sometimes I just didn't want to hear it. The more photos I saw and the more I remembered how special he was, it would stir up the pain all over again. I guess I was just wanting to hide from reality. For the first year or so, I just had to muscle through all this, but I was loving and patient with Jill and others who received much healing through the memories.

That even went for Beau's music. Although he was an amazing producer, singer, and songwriter, it was so hard for me to listen to his songs at first, because once more it magnified my loss and the pain in my soul. But it meant so much to his sisters! Even to this day, as much as I love to hear his music creations, it still has a two-edged-sword effect on my heart— blessing me and hurting me at the same time. But I don't mind the hurt because I enjoy his music so much, and it connects me with him in a special way. Similarly now in this season of my life, I am also extremely blessed when anyone shows me a picture or mentions Beau or his music in any way. But it certainly wasn't always this way for me!

OTHERS ARE HURTING TOO

Even as a husband and wife must work on being tender and patient with each other, you must also show copious amounts of grace and love to your surviving children and extended family members. They have also sustained an unbearable casualty and must be treated with respect and patience in their journey.

In the beginning, I was so centered on my own pain and loss, at first I didn't realize how much others were also struggling, besides of course Jill and our beautiful daughters.

The whole thing was so hard on our parents and siblings, as well as our close friends, our children's best friends, and of course Beau's cousins and friends. There were so many people hurting and confused over this bombshell that had exploded, and at first I just didn't see it.

Many of them were as confused as we were about how this could happen to us, especially since we were "the strong Christians and ministers" in the family. So many looked up to us and admired our walk with God and our faith. And now this? How could it be? *How could it happen to them?*

There was so much hurt in every direction, and to be honest I didn't realize it at first because I was so focused on the personal survival of our immediate family. We all had our individual journeys of pain and remorse, with our daughters loving their little brother more than words can express. Most do not realize how they have stumbled along in their lives, marriages, and raising their children with this thorn in their side the entire way, "limping" at times and hoping for some help to heal their broken hearts.

We all looked to God and did what we could, but each one of us had to find our own way through this valley of pain. Of course we loved each other and did our best to comfort and console one other, but, again, it is such a personal journey. I recently read a scripture which explained it really well: *"Don't expect anyone else to fully understand both the bitterness and the joys of all you experience in your life."* (Proverbs 14:10 TPT)

In other words, no one can *really* understand the depth of your grief and pain, so don't expect them to, because in reality, unless they have experienced loss on the level that you have, they can never fully understand, and that's OK. I think this is a very healthy way to look at things.

Some experiences in life are very deep and personal and meant to be between you and the Lord. So don't waste your energy trying to explain some things that just won't be understood in the long run. Keep it precious between you and the Lord. He certainly understands your grief and pain like no one else and He will walk with *you* through your journey of grief and recovery. And when others are uncomfortable around you, wanting you to get over it and move on, He stays close: "*For He Himself has said, 'I will never leave you nor forsake you.' So we may boldly say: 'The Lord is my helper; I will not fear. What can man do to me?'*" (Hebrews 13:5–6)

You walk with me through valleys when I'm overwhelmed
You carry me when my heart is faint
You understand my weakness and cover me with strength
With love You surround me again
You cover me with mercy when no one understands
My bleeding heart in Your loving hands
You gather all of my tears in a holy place
What would I do without Your embrace?
You've carried me through trial and
You've carried me through pain
and in my darkest hour You gave strength to me again
I am so thankful, Lord, for all You are to me.[9]

—"So Thankful," by Jill LeBlanc,
from the album *Your Love Remains*

CHAPTER FIVE

The Analysis of Paralysis

*I am in anguish, always in tears, and I'm worn out with weeping.
I'm becoming old because of grief; my health is broken.*

—Psalm 31:9 TPT

Something that often accompanies traumatic loss is the added dysfunction of paralysis—not always, but certainly it does for many, including myself (Jill).

The shock of losing a close, very-loved one can render a person helpless in many ways, basically paralyzed from the head to the heart! They have trouble thinking clearly, can't make decisions, have trouble sleeping, become reclusive, and develop poor judgment. For some it is in the tumultuous days and weeks just following the loss. For others, it can carry on for months. Rabbi Earl Grollman writes, "Your sensibilities are numbed. You feel as if you are under anesthesia. Because of this numbness, you do not feel everything at once; you have not wholly absorbed the grim reality of the death of your loved one."[10]

What used to be a no-brainer suddenly leaves them lost, even confused and emotionally immobile. We're not necessarily referring to memory issues, but trauma can certainly affect one's memory going forward. It's decision-making for simple things like where to go eat, or what to eat. Or, "Do I even *want* to eat?!" Some completely lose their appetite for a time.

It's the extreme awkwardness of being around people who don't understand and not being able to express themselves, so they say nothing.

It's, "I want to go for a drive but I don't want to leave the house," and if they go, they might even get lost by driving in a daze.

The day of Beau's memorial in St. Louis, I recall standing in my closet paralyzed, looking at all my clothes and saying, "What do I wear to my son's funeral?! Screw it! I don't want to do this!!" There in the closet alone, I sobbed gut-wrenching tears and I literally wanted to just run away from all of it! But to where?

As time to leave for the service was too quickly approaching, I finally grabbed the only thing that seemed appealing—my gray skinny jeans folded on the shelf, as well as my orange poncho. Not sure I ever wore them together before that day or since, and who says a mother can't wear jeans to her son's funeral? You just do what you have to in these traumatic moments. *And that's okay.*

The Bible is very clear about helping the helpless:

You must defend those who are helpless and have no hope. (Proverbs 31:9 CEV)

This is what someone becomes because of grief-induced paralysis. Even though they may not realize they will need assistance with certain things, gently insist on just coming and "being there" for them.

Two days later, this same type of paralysis almost costed us dearly.

Because of the number of family and friends who lived in Phoenix at the time, including Charlie's elderly parents, we felt it only right to hold another service there. Our friend Brenda had graciously made arrangements for us with a wonderful church, and our local family in the area did the rest of the planning. It was all such a huge blessing. That one was scheduled for Thursday, after the St. Louis service on Monday, which meant flying on Wednesday.

But I became so paralyzed in my mind that we almost missed our flight!

I began on Tuesday to try and pack for this trip. I could not think what to do, and I've been a business traveler for years (I could practically pack blindfolded and mindlessly, prior to this). Thankfully the laundry was already done. I had folded it the night before while lifelong girlfriends who were there to support us hung out in our bedroom with me since the house was *full* of other friends and acquaintances following the funeral.

Tuesday morning I stood in the closet and just stared at my clothing hanging there, silently starring back as if to taunt me! I didn't know what to do. I *could not* think what to do. So I walked away to try again later. But later never came. Although it hung over me all day, I just could not make myself pack anything. I was paralyzed.

All this time was peppered with outbreaks of tears and mourning, sometimes merely wells of hot tears streaming down my face, and other times unexpected and uncontrolled sobbing, interspersed with waves of anger. It just became commonplace.

But when Wednesday morning came, we had a plane to catch.

It was nice to see the sun shining again, tattling on me by showing all the streaks in the windows I thought were clean. The funeral on Monday was a cloudy, blustery, bone-chilling January day in Missouri—the kind where you just want to curl up in front of a crackling fireplace for hours, trying to shake off the chill. We were all so relieved to not have a graveside service to endure, which would've been like pouring salt in a wound. Wednesday was still very cold yet also pretty and sunny, which is always a welcomed midwinter reprieve to reassure one that at least the Earth is still alive and well.

Once more, I walked into my closet to try my darndest to pack for this dreaded trip. And once again I just stood there.

And the clock was ticking. I began to feel overwhelm take control.

My mother, God bless her, was in the kitchen cleaning up some things. My parents were at a loss for what to do. They, for one, had never lost a grandchild before, and didn't really know how to sufficiently comfort their child. So they just came over and "did." They cleaned, puttered, ran errands, made food, just whatever they could do. And right now, for the first time in my adult life, I needed my momma.

I remember running into the kitchen sobbing and blubbering, "I can't do this! I just can't do this!" and fell into her arms. She just held me and patted my back, and softly said, through her own tears and gritted teeth, "Yes, you can. Yes, you can. You *have* to," as I continued to sob. Those few special moments gave me the strength I needed to go back to my room and try once again to pack.

We barely made it to the flight in time, but we did, and I'm so thankful.

Looking back, I'm so extremely grateful my mother did not try to "fix me." She simply loved me and did what she could to remedy this situation at hand.

While I (Charlie) was reading through our writing and reliving the *pain* we experienced, I sat amazed that we have come this far. This was the deepest, darkest moment of our lives, our hearts were shattered and our breath was taken away. But somehow, through God's loving hand and grace, we made it through and are now able to breathe again. That's amazing. Actually, *Amazing Grace!*

> *Yea, though I walk through the valley of the shadow of death, I will fear no evil; For You are with me.* (Psalm 23:4)

I (Jill) was beyond heartbroken to hear the husband of my childhood friend passed away very suddenly in his mid-sixties. It left Linda in a tumult of shock, mourning, grief and, for months, almost insurmountable paralysis. Sadly, their financial situation was not prepared for such a tragedy, leaving her and their son also completely crushed, in a seemingly impossible scenario of survival.

She had her own business that contributed to the household income, but only a small percentage of what her husband would bring home, which was now suddenly gone.

And worse, *he* was gone.

Her world stopped. She lived in a blur—a nightmare she could never wake up from.

She began having panic attacks and continual flashbacks of attempting CPR on their bathroom floor until EMTs finally arrived. She was unable to sleep at night. Her jaw locked up as a result of the trauma and she couldn't open it for weeks to eat solid food.

For months, any car driving by on their quiet street she would think was him coming home from work, but he never again walked through that door. Mike was gone and he was not coming back.

She prayed and cried… a lot! Many well-meaning friends and family did their best to step up and try to help—take care of the yard, send gift cards for meals out, send money, and, *oh my*—the plants she received were enough to start a floral business. Now she had all those to take care of—but most of them eventually died too. It was just too much, being in a paralyzed state of mind.

Thankfully she and her son made it through those dreadful early days, weeks, and months, as difficult as they were. In reality you don't think you can make it through another day, but somehow you do.

You are in shock. Nothing seems real. You are not there. People talk to you; you do not respond. You fear as though you are just a spectator. There is a deadening of feeling. You have lost your ability to concentrate. You have no energy. There is a slowdown in your speech, in the way you move. You are literally stunned. These are signs of a temporary paralysis…you have not wholly absorbed the grim reality of the death of your loved one.[11]

One of Beau's very close friends, Jesse, passed away suddenly and tragically nine years after Beau left. On the morning of the memorial service, his momma, who has always been so organized and detailed, the one who has forever served others with such grace—including us so beautifully in our own time of mourning—was now suddenly lost. The service was quickly approaching, and not only did she have to go get herself ready, but she wasn't able to direct us in the tasks of gathering the items needed at the venue, so we just jumped in and took over, taking all that off her plate. Paralysis from grief is just so mind-numbing for the simplest of duties.

As difficult as this is, especially early on, we are *so* thankful to God for His unending love and help! The Bible says He is a very present help in time of need (Psalm 46:1). He certainly was for us, and I know He has been for so many who have also walked through this. I also know He will be there for *you*, if you are experiencing this numbness after your loss.

Don't try to be a superhero. If you need to cry, please allow yourself. If you need to stop and just sit down for a moment, do it. Wait to do some of the things others are expecting of you. You don't have to clean out your loved one's clothes and personal things right away. Who says there is a timeline for these things? You do it at your own pace when you have the strength and the heart to handle it. It will never be easy, but maybe later will be easier than now. Wait it out until you gain enough strength for these types of tasks. As a wise minister shared with us, "Be kind to yourself."

They who wait for the Lord shall renew their strength;
they shall mount up with wings like eagles; they shall run
and not be weary; they shall walk and not faint.
(Isaiah 40:31 ESV)

(Dedicated to Linda and Dustin.)

Earth has no sorrow that Heaven can't heal

Though we seem broken and scarred

Hope for tomorrow and strength for today

Always embraced in His arms

Always embraced in His arms[12]

—"God of All Comfort," by Charlie & Jill LeBlanc,
from the album *Your Love Remains*

CHAPTER SIX

Understanding Grief

*I am dying of grief; my years are shortened by sadness.
...I am wasting away from within.*

—Psalm 31:10 NLT

---

grief—noun. Deep mental anguish, as that
arising from bereavement, or an instance of
this. A source or cause of deep mental anguish.
Annoyance or frustration, or an instance of this.
Trouble or difficulty, or an instance of this.[13]

grieve—transitive verb. To sorrow over; deplore;
lament. To feel grief; be in mental distress;
sorrow; mourn, to feel very sad about.[14]

My own (Jill's) simple definition of grief is, "Deep sorrow,
especially caused by someone's death, or the death of
something." Other synonyms found in the dictionary for
"grieve" are *agonize, anguish, distress, bleed, hurt, mourn,
sorrow, suffer.*[15]

These synonyms are *real* emotions that take place in the heart of someone walking through a devastating loss, and are part of the pain that many people struggle through. Yet grief is more than emotion. It is a season, almost an uninvited "chaperone," accompanying us through the time of readjusting our lives following a deep loss. Rabbi Earl Grollman points out, "Grief is unbearable heartache, sorrow, loneliness. Because you loved, grief walks by your side. Grief is one of the most basic of human emotions. Grief is very, very normal."[16]

Grief, accompanied with deep sorrow and tears, is something that is hard to talk about and explain, but, unfortunately it is a common occurrence, living on this side of Heaven. Grief or separation is something we, as God's children, were never supposed to experience. He created us to live forever in continual fellowship with Him, never dying or having to endure losing a loved one to death. But all that changed when Adam and Eve broke fellowship with God and handed over their authority to the enemy.

Enter: the pain of loss.

Make no mistake about it, friends, when our boy passed away and we felt that pain of loss, *we grieved*, and a lot!! Yes, we are born again, Spirit-filled graduates of Rhema Bible Training College, full-time ministers, teachers, songwriters, and worship leaders for more than forty years, having the privilege to work with two of the greatest Bible teachers in our generation along with many other amazing pastors and teachers. But we still grieved the loss of our son, and we grieved long and hard.

We had *numerous* times (too many to count) of *very* deep sorrow and uncontrollable tears. The pain of losing our sweet son was like a tearing and ripping of our souls! As time went on, we became stronger, but it was a V–E–R–Y S–L–O–W process.

Even with all the grief and mourning, there was a hope holding our hearts, the hope of glory, *Jesus*—and the great hope of knowing we will be with our son again.

But aren't we as believers *not* supposed to grieve?

Let's look at this scripture together. Paul said, *"And now, dear brothers and sisters, we want you to know what will happen to the believers who have died so you will not grieve like people who have no hope."* (1 Thessalonians 4:13 NLT)

It's so great that Paul addressed this, since there was now a new paradigm to embrace: Jesus' resurrection opened the gates of Heaven wide, to receive the departed believers straight into the presence of the Lord! This established a completely different understanding of grieving the loss of our loved ones.

Now, note that Paul did *not* say we are to not grieve. He said we should not grieve like people who have no hope— unbelievers with no hope of Heaven or eternal life with Jesus— in other words, hopelessly. Have you ever met someone like that? They are beyond miserable and distraught! What a *horrible* journey that would be to live out!

Thankfully, we don't grieve like those who don't know Him! We can still experience sorrow, but in a different way, knowing we will one day be reunited.

As intense as our sorrow was early on, it cannot be compared with the sorrow of those who don't know the Lord, with no hope of ever seeing their loved one again. I cannot even imagine how people who do not know Jesus survive this type of pain, or even those who aren't sure of their loved one's salvation. Our hearts deeply go out to them!

We thank God that as believers we *do* have the hope of seeing our loved one again! And what a comfort to know that even right now, our son is blessed and full of joy, way beyond our comprehension.

We have had, and do have hope regarding our son:

Jesus, our hope of glory,
the living hope of eternal life,
and the hope and assurance of reuniting in Heaven,
where we'll be together f-o-r-e-v-e-r.

As King David said of his son, *"I will go to him, but he will not return to me."* (2 Samuel 12:23 NIV)

But even with knowing all this, *we struggled* over our loss and the pain of separation.

I (Charlie) wrote this in my journal, three years after Beau's departure:

So what I am trying to say is, losing a loved one, especially a child, is like you get cut deeply and something is ripped out of you. Like, you have an accident and one of your internal organs is ripped out of you, or like a part of your heart is torn out of you. Maybe you survive the accident but you are missing a vital part. And on top of it you have a very serious wound which is very PAINFUL and needs TIME to HEAL! Healing is a process, and during that process there are painful days. Then sometimes you begin to heal and the doctor has to reopen the wound, which alone is painful, and then work on trying to remove infection, which is also painful. And then some days, healing itself just HURTS.

In many cases, there is a process of healing in the soul, getting through some of this tough stuff, which many times *is not instant.* For Jill and for me, it took a lot of T-I-M-E. And I know for a fact, *many* godly, faith-filled men and women who have experienced tragic loss say the same thing.

One of the main aspects of Jesus' ministry was to heal the brokenhearted. This proves how broken hearts are universal and need Jesus for healing. Jesus said: *"The Spirit of the* Lord *is upon Me, because He has anointed Me to preach the gospel to the poor; He has sent Me to heal the brokenhearted."* (Luke 4:18)

Please open your soul and allow Jesus to begin bringing healing to your broken heart, even if you don't understand it all. He loves you so much, and cares for you so deeply.

Healing takes time, especially when it comes to an unexpected, untimely death. Your soul is ripped open as your loved one is ripped from you, and this kind of jagged wound takes T-I-M-E to heal.

Proverbs 13:12 confirms,

Hope deferred makes the heart sick.

And look at this from the Good News Translation,

When hope is crushed, the heart is crushed.

But we then remember what the psalmist David also said,

He restores my soul. (Psalm 23:3)

I'm reminded again of the scripture passages from the famous song "Great is Thy Faithfulness." It ministered to me so much when I read what Jeremiah said in the scriptures just before he declares God's faithfulness (which we quoted earlier):

I cry out, "My splendor is gone!
Everything I had hoped for from the Lord is lost!"
The thought of my suffering …
is bitter beyond words.
I will never forget this awful time,
as I grieve over my loss.
Yet I still dare to hope
when I remember this:

The faithful love of the Lord never ends!

His mercies never cease.

Great is His faithfulness;

His mercies begin afresh each morning.

(Lamentations 3:20–23 NLT)

Oh, how we relate so much to this passage! It really shares our testimony in a nutshell. Everything we had hoped for was lost, but we remembered (and have experienced) the love of the Lord and His faithfulness to carry us and heal our broken hearts.

We are *so thankful* to God for *His* restoration in our lives, and for what He will do in yours (and hopefully has already begun).

As we look more deeply into the scriptures about the subject of loss, grief, sorrow and mourning, we see how it was a common thread of Earth-life in this broken world we live in. Even Jesus, along with many great men and women of God, experienced grief.

For example in the garden of Gethsemane, when Jesus was facing the cross and about to bear the sin and sickness of the world, He lamented,

My soul is very sad and deeply grieved, so that I am almost dying of sorrow. (Matthew 26:38 AMP)

Luke shows another side of this horrific moment:

Being in agony He prayed more earnestly; and His sweat became like great drops of blood falling down to the ground. (Luke 22:44)

In another instance we see Jesus weeping over the city of Jerusalem. (Luke 19:41)

After He heard of his cousin John being executed, Jesus left by boat to go be alone in a remote place. (Matthew 14:13)

Yes, Jesus understands grief:

He was despised and rejected by men, a Man of sorrows and pain and acquainted with grief. (Isaiah 53:3 AMP)

Even the great apostle Paul said in speaking of his beloved companion, Epaphroditus:

He certainly was sick and close to death. But God had mercy on him, and not only on him but also on me, so that I would not have sorrow upon sorrow. (Philippians 2:27 AMP)

Paul clearly stated he would have had "sorrow upon sorrow" had Epaphroditus died! We all agree Paul was a very spiritual man of God, yet he was admitting just how difficult it would have been, and he would have had intense sorrow—a perfect example of grief and mourning.

Paul also said:

My heart is filled with bitter sorrow and unending grief for my people. (Romans 9:2–3 NLT)

Mourning over the loss of a loved one is not unspiritual or ungodly:

Godly men buried Stephen and **mourned deeply** for him. (Acts 8:2 NIV)

And then we see others:

~ David, the king, mighty warrior and psalmist, lifting his voice and weeping at the grave of his son Abner. (2 Samuel 3:31–32)

~ Abraham mourned and wept for his wife Sarah. (Genesis 23:2)

~ Joseph fell on his father's face and wept for his father, Jacob. (Genesis 50:1–3)

As we can see through these passages and many more, sorrow and grief are *normal* responses in painful situations, even for *godly* men and women. You just cannot place all sadness in one box and label it all as weakness or self-pity.

The point is, many wonderful, godly, strong believers will grieve when they lose a loved one, and they should. We must give them space for this *and* keep in mind, this is not wrong, but rather a very healthy, biblical, God-given response, almost like a vent, to release pressure for the sake of our souls.

Jesus said He came to heal the brokenhearted and comfort those who mourn, *not* condemn or rebuke them. In fact, as you will see often mentioned in these pages, scripture says to **weep with** *those who weep*, not rebuke or try to correct those who weep (Romans 12:15)!

Dr. Colin Murray Parkes, in his book, *Bereavement: Studies of Grief in Adult Life*, says it this way: "The pain of grief is just as much part of life as the joy of love: It is perhaps *the price we pay for love,* the cost of commitment. To ignore this fact, or to pretend that it is not so, is to put on emotional blinkers [or blinders] which leave us unprepared for the losses that will inevitably occur in our own lives, and unprepared to help others cope with losses in theirs."[17]

Rabbi Grollman says this: "Grief is not a disorder, a disease or a sign of weakness. It is an emotional, physical and spiritual necessity, [and quotes Dr. Parkes] the price you pay for love."[18] We certainly have experienced that cost of love. There are *still* times on occasion when our souls become sad, our eyes well with tears, or we may even cry hard, depending on what tender places in our hearts were prodded by something—a memory, a photo, hearing from someone who misses Beau, seeing his possessions we still have, hearing his music, or many other reminders. Yes, even years later. And it's usually when we least expect it!

So, please understand:

WE

    STILL

        GRIEVE,

and so do so many who have lost loved ones, even though you may not notice because we hide it well (sometimes). Thankfully, the Lord's loving kindnesses indeed never cease, and He is always faithful to come alongside and bring help and comfort, even years later.

Here is another super helpful excerpt He led us to:

Grief doesn't come and go in an orderly, confined time frame. Just when we think the pangs of anguish have stolen their last breath, another wave sweeps in and we are forced to revisit the memories, the pain, the fear. Sometimes we try to resist the demands of grieving. We long to avoid this fierce, yet holy pilgrimage. We fight against the currents, terrified of being overwhelmed, of being discovered, of becoming lost in our brokenness...

Yet grief, as painful a season as it is, is a necessary part of our healing. To run from grief is to run from the very thing that can quell the pain of our loss. If we come to God and use Bible verses and prayer for healing, our grief has a purpose. Grieving is the process God uses to bring us to a place of wholeness.[19]

And most importantly, our Savior Jesus has this to say:

Come to Me, all you who are weary and burdened, and I will give you rest. Take My yoke upon you and learn from Me, for I am gentle and humble in heart, and "you will find rest for your souls." For My yoke is easy and My burden is light. (Matthew 11:28–30 TLV)

Words can't express how extremely grateful we are for the Lord's continual love and kindness to us through these years. There is no way on Earth we would have recovered to this point without Him. And to be sure, our dearest friends and godly ministers who were patient with us, loved us, wept with us, and comforted us, without question were and still are an important part of our healing journey. *Thank you!*

We put our hope in You,

You are our help and shield

Our hearts rejoice in You,

We trust Your holy name

Your unfailing love surrounds us,

We put our hope in You alone

With your favor You have crowned us

Your love remains above everything.

—*"Your Love Remains,"* by Charlie LeBlanc,
from the album *Your Love Remains*[20]

A Time for Tears

To everything there is a season,
a time for every purpose under heaven:
…A time to weep, and a time to laugh;
a time to mourn, and a time to dance.

—Ecclesiastes 3:1, 4

Some look at grief and crying as synonyms, or basically the same thing. But, as we've mentioned, grief is not only an emotion, but more of a time or season one walks through when they experience loss on a deep level. It comes in waves, and often seemingly out of nowhere, when you aren't expecting it! And for many, for a *long* time.

Crying accompanies grief sometimes, but not all the time. You can grieve deeply in your heart without crying.

After our son Beau died, we both experienced uncontrollable times of crying. Our hearts just could not hold the pain and sorrow we were experiencing, so we let it out with wailing and tears. I (Charlie) wasn't sure what was happening to me, finding myself crying several times a day. For months!

I read books, emailed and called minister friends who had lost children, and asked for help because I was desperate to know how to make it through this and keep my sanity and faith. I even went to my doctor, who also knew our son, asking for help. Thankfully, instead of throwing antidepressants at me, he wisely encouraged me that what I was experiencing was very normal for this kind of trauma, and I would get through it—eventually.

I was also spiritually aware that the enemy was trying to take us out completely. I recalled Proverbs 4:23, *"Guard your heart above all else, for it determines the course of your life"* (NLT). I knew my life and my future hinged on how my heart would get through this. As the saying goes, through life's hardships you can become bitter or better, and I wanted to be better!

Thankfully, in my search, I came across an article by Tony Cooke called "It's Okay to Cry," and it all started making sense. I finally found a godly, faith-filled Bible teacher who understood what I was feeling and experiencing, and had written about it:

> *People working through grief have learned that it takes time to process certain emotions. Don't become frustrated and discouraged with yourself if you find that it's taking you longer than you would like. Even though you make decisions and endeavor to live by those decisions, it can still take considerable time to regain*

spiritual and emotional equilibrium following a significant loss.[21]

How can it be so wrong to cry when there's just no way to stop it? This brought *massive* comfort, and showed us tears are not so much a sign of weakness or a lack of faith as some may think, but a normal reaction stemming from some of life's pains. We also learned our tears were a natural expression of the depths of love we had for our son, now departed.

In fact, a friend who lost his daughter emailed me with these comforting words after our loss, *"Emotions are the essence of relationship."*

This said to me, the more we love, the more we hurt emotionally when they are gone.

We also learned that our tears are precious to God. He doesn't condemn us when we are crying or mourning the loss of our beloved, instead He is right there with us.

You keep track of all my sorrows. You have collected all my tears in your bottle. You have recorded each one in your book. (Psalm 56:8 NLT)

I thank God for this truth, because we all, as family and friends, were crying buckets of tears for several years, and even some still to this day. And that's okay.

Washington Irving, a famous American writer is credited with this insight:

There is a sacredness in tears. They are not the mark of weakness, but of power. They speak more eloquently than ten thousand tongues. They are the messengers of overwhelming grief, of deep contrition, and of unspeakable love.[22]

Before we lost our son, we really had no idea what grief was and didn't understand people who were experiencing it. We were always compassionate toward those who were hurting, but I just could not grasp what they were feeling or experiencing.

But following Beau's death and after many days of uncontrollable tears, I understood.

Notice Jesus' heart as He was approaching the tomb of His friend Lazarus, and saw his sisters Mary and Martha,

When Jesus saw her weeping, and the Jews who came with her weeping, He groaned in the spirit and was troubled. And He said, "Where have you laid him?"

They said to Him, "Lord, come and see."

Jesus wept. (John 11:33–35)

This passage is well known as the shortest scripture in the Bible, yet very powerful. It blessed me beyond words, knowing I was not alone in this pool of tears.

Some may think Jesus was weeping because of their unbelief, but really, *He wept* because of love.

See how He loved him. (John 11:36)

Jesus loved Lazarus, and He loved Mary and Martha. They had become close friends by this time. He hated watching them go through this pain and suffering.

The Scripture says,

He is touched with the feeling of our infirmities.
(Hebrews 4:15 KJV)

Yes, He was touched and very troubled by the pain in humanity and the things we go through in this fallen world.

Let's unpack this thought a little bit:

"Touched" is the Greek word *sumpatheó*, also defined as,

1. *to be affected with the same feeling as another, to sympathize with*

2. *to feel for, have compassion on.*[23]

"Infirmities" is also translated "weaknesses."

So we can also read it like this: "He is touched, affected, and feels the feelings of our weaknesses!"

We also read that Paul told us to *"weep with those who weep."* (Romans 12:15)

That's exactly what Jesus was doing with the friends He loved. It dawned on me how God, through His Word, would never ask us to do anything Jesus would not do; therefore, I believe Jesus weeps with those who weep, especially when mourning over loss.

In fact Isaiah 63:9 says, *"In all their suffering he also suffered, and he personally rescued them."* (NLT)

Some think if you shed tears, the Lord looks down on you for lack of faith. But really, when we suffer He also suffers, and when we weep He also weeps. He is touched with our weaknesses and He is close to the brokenhearted. Even when you feel alone and like no one understands, He's right there with you, holding you close. He's so wonderful and gracious!

> *The Lord is close to the brokenhearted; He rescues those whose spirits are crushed.* (Psalm 34:18 NLT)

> *The Lord is compassionate and merciful, slow to get angry and filled with unfailing love.* (Psalm 103:8 NLT)

It is not ungodly to have sorrow and even shed tears when you are missing someone you love.

Remember the story of Joseph being sold into slavery by his brothers and years later becoming second in command of all Egypt? He then sees his beloved younger brother Benjamin, his own mother's son, for the first time in many years!

> *Joseph hurried from the room because he was overcome with emotion for his brother. He went into his private room, where he broke down and wept.* (Genesis 43:30 NLT)

> *And then when he revealed himself to all his brothers, he broke down and wept so loudly, the Egyptians could hear him.* (Genesis 45:1–2)

This was not weakness, it was *love*. The more you love, the more it hurts when you experience separation.

We then see David mourning deeply with tears at the death of his son Absalom,

The king was overcome with emotion. He went up to the room over the gateway and burst into tears. And as he went, he cried, "O my son Absalom! My son, my son Absalom! If only I had died instead of you! O Absalom, my son, my son." (2 Samuel 18:33 NLT)

(We know what this is like!)

Then look at David and his mighty army of men arriving home to Ziklag, seeing their town had been raided and their wives and children taken by the enemy. It then says they wept until they could weep no more. (1 Samuel 30:3–4)

(We also know what *this* is like!)

These men were not weak or even unspiritual. This is a normal expression of hearts being torn and broken over the loss of their loved ones! (Thank God, later their families were rescued.)

We pray this helps you to release yourself to cry if you need to. God never looks down on these emotions; in fact, He gave them to us for these very moments. We've encountered some who are actually afraid to let themselves mourn and cry, for fear that would not be "in faith" and would spiral down into a deep, dark hole and never be able to pull out of it. We found it was important to try and always keep Jesus in the middle of our sorrows, and cry out to Him in our grief, and this may help you as well.

This reminds me of a very difficult moment in my (Charlie's) journey.

Following both of Beau's memorial services, we had been away in San Diego for a month. After returning, it was time to revisit Beau's apartment in Scottsdale to clean out all his clothes and belongings. Man, this was extremely heart-wrenching: To touch his very cool clothes, his music equipment, his jewelry—all of it was so painful. We finally got everything into our car and stored at my brother's house for a couple of days until we could pack up everything and ship to our home in St. Louis.

The day came to box up all his music books of songs and poems he had written, along with books and notes from the recording engineering school he had attended. Add to that his music gear, drums, and studio equipment.

Something began to well up in my heart as I was overcome with pain and grief. I screamed out with anguish and wept like I hadn't in weeks. (I thought I was alone in my brother's house at that moment—but Jill was downstairs and heard me.) The pain of seeing all his music, life, and dreams being thrown into a box—it just all caved in on me that afternoon. The connection I had with Beau and his music had been ripped out of my soul. I wept bitterly, harder than I had ever wept before.

It reminds me of Jeremiah 31:15: "A cry is heard in Ramah—deep anguish and bitter weeping. Rachel weeps for her children, refusing to be comforted—for her children are gone." (NLT)

It was horrible, but yet a very holy moment. I don't quite know how to accurately describe it. There was pain, heart-wrenching grief, cleansing, and freedom all at the same time. It was like journeying through a tunnel or passage I had to go through. I didn't want to but knew I had to—there was no way out, except through.

Jill tells of a similar experience several months later:

We were finally home from most of our traveling during that first summer after Beau left us in January. One warm afternoon I (Jill) walked into the garage looking for something, and searched everywhere I could to locate the item.

I came across a set of those cheap plastic drawers thinking, Hmmm. What's in here? I opened one and was shocked to find several pieces of Beau's clothing. It was as if a flurry of moths flew up into my face! I recall being so startled that I flinched and gasped, then immediately broke out deeply sobbing, hardly being able to catch my breath until the grief subsided and I could breathe again.

Some of you may have experienced this same gut-wrenching reality in your journey. If so, our hearts are with you. It can be so, so hard, especially early on.

So here's a question: Is it unspiritual, showing weakness to break down in tears like that, or is it possibly a healing balm to the soul? We believe letting your heart "bleed" like this can be a helpful, healthy response to a difficult situation, although at the moment it may seem just the opposite.

Sometimes you just need a good cry to get through a tough situation like this. And then another. And eventually *another*. Unfortunately, some feel they cannot express themselves through tears or let themselves cry, and they become bound up, dysfunctional, and never fully get through their pain.

To the contrary, tears can be healing and cleansing. Letting yourself cry can definitely release pent-up emotion and bring a feeling of release, even though it may only be momentary. Like physical exercise, which is also hard, it may cause pain for a while, but without it you will never get stronger. Similarly, if you do not allow yourself to outwardly grieve and mourn, even though you may only do it in private, you will delay and even hinder your recovery, making it hard to grow stronger.

Rabbi Grollman had this to say about it:

The time to grieve is NOW. Do not suppress or ignore your mourning reactions. If you do, your feelings will be like smoldering embers, which may later ignite and cause a more dangerous explosion.[24]

Grief after loss is an interesting journey, with many twists, turns, and a life of its own. Therefore we believe it is important for people to have the freedom to express their grief *without any fear or condemnation of what others might think.*

If you have experienced a heartbreak or the loss of a loved one and haven't let yourself "go there" for fear of showing weakness, please be free from that ungodly bondage!

God will wipe away every tear from their eyes; there shall be no more death, nor sorrow, nor crying. There shall be no more pain, for the former things have passed away. (Revelation 21:4)

The Bible instructs us to *"Rejoice with those who rejoice, and weep with those who weep"* (Romans 12:15). It's really easy to rejoice with someone who shares something great with you: They've just gotten engaged, are pregnant, got a raise, a job, a good report from the doctor, passed a test, and the like.

But how about when someone experiences devastation, like loss? Or divorce? Or financial disaster? We on the outside want to cower and hide, because we don't know what to say or do and are afraid to bring up the loss, lest it "remind them" of their sorrow. *Trust me—they have not forgotten.*

C. S. Lewis likened it to a man losing his leg—he *never* forgets the stump during daily routines—getting up or down, showering, dressing, walking—it's just always there. And yet others who only see him out and about wearing his prosthetic don't realize the struggle he endures on a daily basis. So it is with losing a close loved one, and some say especially a child. We are *constantly* reminded our loved ones are gone (or whatever the loss), even in living ordinary, everyday life!

But weeping with those who weep is one of the most loving, caring and comforting things you can do with your hurting friend. Be assured—it is a treasure that will live on in the heart of the griever. We hate to see someone else suffer on our behalf, but for some crazy reason, there is something *very* heartwarming and enriching for the bereaved to know others care enough to hurt with us. This is "bearing one another's burdens" in the truest sense of the word. We don't want others to be pained at our expense, but there is healing in it, nonetheless.

> *Carry each other's burdens, and in this way you will fulfill the law of Christ.* (Galatians 6:2 NIV)

And what is the law of Christ? It's *love*, like Jesus spoke about in John 13:34. "Love" is a verb—an *action* word, not a feeling. And showing this type of action will bring a layer of healing in someone's broken heart.

Grief is painful. It *really* hurts. Deep down. And for most, it hurts a long time.

Let us affirm you—it's okay to cry. And always remember, *your* tears before God are precious. He saves them. He loves you and has compassion on you. He understands your pain and will minister to you. He comforts those who mourn.

> *Blessed are those who mourn, for they shall be comforted.* (Matthew 5:4)

In closing, let's again ponder this wonderful passage that validates our discussion:

All praises belong to the God and Father of our Lord Jesus Christ. For He is the Father of tender mercy and the God of endless comfort. He always comes alongside us to comfort us in every suffering so that we can come alongside those who are in any painful trial. We can bring them this same comfort that God has poured out upon us. (2 Corinthians 1:3–4 TPT)

PART 2

To the one whose loved one is gone from this life:

So far we've shared some insights of what those walk through whose lives have been turned upside down through loss. We pray if this is you, you will have received courage, affirmation and hope to believe you will survive this onslaught in your life. But don't stop here—there is more affirmation to be had in the coming chapters!

To the one walking beside:

As one walking with them through this journey, YOU are here with them at this moment in time, and God wants to use you to bring peace and comfort to your grieving friend. As we continue sharing more about the different kinds of loss, the devastation brought to the one left behind, and things that do and don't help, we believe you will have a heart to learn how to be a better help and a blessing to them. In time, you will make a positive difference in their lives, and assist them to regain their footing, maybe a little more easily!

CHAPTER EIGHT

Losing a Sibling
and Other Close Loved Ones

How I weep for you, my brother Jonathan!
Oh, how much I loved you!

—2 Samuel 1:26, NLT

Our daughters lost their little brother. Their only brother and *very* close friend. He was warm, funny (hilarious, actually), caring, friend of the underdog and the overlooked, and seemed to light up a room when he walked in. He had no shortage of very close friends, which included many cousins. But I would say, those who loved him most (besides us) were his two sisters.

Camille and Cherrie suffered a devastating blow.

In the aftermath of Beau's death, one thing that broke our hearts over and over was seeing the pain Beau's sisters encountered, which was rarely acknowledged by others. Generally, people were so loving and caring toward *us*, his parents, but seldom did they inquire how our daughters were faring. Not never, but rarely.

It seems siblings of the departed often go unnoticed in their suffering. I (Jill) was hoping others were stepping up to reach out and continue showing love, sympathy and compassion to them, but unfortunately I only occasionally heard that someone would. I think *everyone* in our world was just hurting so badly, they *all* needed someone to reach out to them as well.

Truth be told, the entire family (and often extended family) is rocked by losing one of its members.

In our family, we all cared for each other so much and didn't want to say anything to cause another wave of grief to overtake the other. Along with this, not only were we living in different states geographically, we each lived in a different relationship with the same person, our son and brother, and each of us grieved differently over the loss. At times we weren't comfortable trying to communicate that pain with each other.

Once the initial clouds of dust settled and life began racing forward in the weeks and months following the funeral, I noticed the girls didn't seem to want to talk much with us about Beau, his illness or his death, or how they were processing. We found it a little unusual. But at the same time, we were the same way toward them and very careful with what we would say. It honestly just became awkward—none of us wanted to cause more pain to the other.

Our daughter Camille writes,

Although we were all missing and grieving the loss of the same person, we were all living in very different spaces with our grief and experiencing very uniquely different feelings and emotions, which maybe we felt the others didn't or couldn't relate to.

At different times throughout our family's collective grief journey, we have each felt the need and burden to be strong, stoic and stable, for the sake of the whole. This of course only left everyone else feeling alone and disconnected in their pain… all the while everyone's heart is bleeding over one person, our beloved Beau.

Eventually we realized what was happening and began to talk freely together about him. This brought a lot of healing, laughter, *and* tears, but it was all very healthy. In some cultures it is actually superstitious to speak of the departed. But, to the contrary, we've found it so important and therapeutic for one to talk about their loved one who has passed on!

We'd like to share some of our daughters' social media posts through the years, just to show a sibling's perspective to the depths of which many do not fully realize or properly acknowledge.

POSTS FROM CHERRIE

Almost four years out:

Shedding tears today in memory of you. Missing you as always, but today more than usual. Wish I could call you and hear one of your smart-ass retorts or some incredibly insane story that you would tell so hilariously well. I'm aching for you today. I love you, always will. xo

Seventh Christmas without him:

As Christmas approaches, it always brings memories of the day you came home from your chemo treatment just a couple weeks before you left us. Wish I had your name on my list of people to buy gifts for this year. I definitely wouldn't mind that at all...

Ninth anniversary of his passing, posted along with a four-person family selfie we took after going to brunch together in Beau's honor, all big smiles on our faces because of the cold, whipping January wind:

Smile, though your heart is aching

Smile, even though it's breaking

When there are clouds in the sky, you'll get by

If you smile through your fear and sorrow

Smile and maybe tomorrow

You'll see the sun come shining through, if you just smile....[25]

#BCL #neverforget #9years #forever5

During the tenth year:

A friend just posted this and it just says everything....(and how true it is!)

"Speak Their Name"

Someone I love has gone away

And life is not the same

The greatest gift that you can give

Is just to speak their name

I need to hear the stories

And the tales of days gone past

I need for you to understand

These memories must last

We cannot make more memories

Since they're no longer here

So when you speak of them to me

It's music to my ears.[26]

#bcl #forevermissedforeverloved #beaucharles
#onefourteentwothousandnine

Eleventh anniversary:

*On one hand, I have all the words. On the other hand,
I have none. It's been eleven years. Eleven. Feels like a
lifetime and a blink of an eye. Today, I wish I could see
his eyes sparkling with mischief one more time, hear his
voice croon a tune one more time, see him chug another
beer one more time. All the things that were Beau. The
hole in my heart doesn't hurt as much some days, and
I'm starting to learn how to live through the pain. Today,
as always, I want to honor his memory by living life to the
fullest, because that's what he did. Each and every day.*

#forevermissedforeverloved #BCL #Boner

POSTS FROM CAMILLE

Beau's twenty-seventh birthday (three and a half years after
he left us):

*Happy Birthday sweet baby bro…loving you…missing
your handsome face, your hugs, your humor, your style,
your spirit, your presence, your voice…Beau you stole
our hearts in the short time that you were here…forever
loved, forever missed, my precious brother! xoxo*

Eighth anniversary:

Your beautiful life, my dear brother, was a blessing…a gift full of inexhaustible passion and joy. The memories of you will forever be my treasure. You were and forever will be loved beyond words…and missed beyond measure. #BCL #livingwithaheartache #rip #legend

Tenth anniversary:

Where there is deep grief, there was great love. I love you, miss you and will mourn your beautiful life forever, my dear precious brother. 💔 *#10years #livingwithabrokenheart #beaucharlesleblanc #bclforever*

Beau's thirty-fourth birthday:

HBD my dear brother…I'll never understand why you're not here today, but it's funny how the older I get, the more I'm reckoning w/the realization that the beauty and loss in this life will forever be beyond my ability to comprehend or understand, at least on this side of Heaven. Nevertheless, I loved you since the day I held you. We've always known each other's hearts, and we were each other's biggest advocates. We shared and celebrated the best of life, and also bore each other's pains and hardships. We cried together, and my god did we laugh!!! We will forever live on, my brother, outside of the touch of time. I love you and I "cheers" to you today. 💔🍰 *#BCL #GNT #irishcarbomb #hbd*

Eleventh anniversary:

Really missing this guy today...actually more like, every single moment of everyday #bestfriend #brother #BCL #11years

Probably nine years or so into the journey, I came across an excellent book which was very poignant in this regard, titled *Surviving the Death of a Sibling*. The author relates the story after losing her adult brother, along with many others' experiences, and describes it this way:

> *Indeed, within days of my brother's death I learned an important lesson. I learned that no matter how paralyzed with grief and sorrow I might have felt, society does not recognize the death of an adult brother or sister as a major loss. Comprehending this, I retreated into the shadows, a place where most other surviving brothers and sisters go to mourn, and waited for the sadness to pass.*
>
> *The sad fact is this: When an adult loses a brother or a sister, society often fails to recognize the depth of such a loss. Witness what I call dismissive condolences, offered by well-intentioned but sorely misguided friends, acquaintances, family members, and coworkers. "Well, you lived in different states, so you probably weren't very close." Or "Thank goodness it wasn't your husband or one of your children." And "Your brother/sister died? How awful! How are your parents?" Intellectually,*

we may understand that people mean well; they're attempting to be helpful and to offer comfort to us in our sorrow. Yet dismissive condolences have the opposite effect. They make our loss seem trivial, and they also make the surviving sibling feel as if his or her grief is somehow unwarranted.[27]

The author also writes of frequently visiting her doctor for anxiety and random ailments, unaware it was all stemming from the trauma of loss. She was chatting with a kind, older gentleman in the waiting room one day and mentioned her brother passed away recently. He then looked down, fiddling with his cane and hesitantly replied, "You never get over losing a brother, you know. You never really get over it."[28]

Doreen lost her only sibling at twenty-one, an older brother whom she loved *so much*. She was sixteen. Growing up in a very dysfunctional home, he was the only safe person and stabilizing force she knew, since they were not Christians at the time. Because of this tragic loss, she spiraled down into a very dark, under-worldly life, almost losing her own life to suicide. Even after becoming born again in her thirties, the deep roots of her delayed grief tried to hold her hostage. Several years later now and completely free from her past, even in her fifties Doreen still finds herself deeply missing and mourning her brother.

In a bizarre accident which eventually led to Gordon's death, Stephen lost his only brother whom he greatly admired. Over twenty years later he *still* mourns at times. Only those who have lost a close sibling can relate to this.

We mentioned our friend dying very unexpectedly. Not only were his wife and son completely devastated from his sudden death, but his sister and brother-in-law were also shocked and broken from this horrible tragedy. And not only this blow, *they* had also lost their nineteen-year-old son more than thirty years earlier in a single-car accident on an icy road late one Christmas Eve, and they never really recovered from it. Now, her only sibling dropped dead, and they were just crushed—injury on top of unhealed injury. I suspect very few have acknowledged all this, which makes the road to recovery so much longer and harder.

One would think, *Well, they* **look** *like they're doing okay, so I don't need to say anything, I'll just pray for them.* Friend, please know your prayers are always welcome! But don't stop there! People generally hide their grief from others, and often no one knows what heartache a sibling often faces.

We must remember the *many people* who are crushed from a loss.

Going forward, when someone you love experiences loss, if at all possible, please remember *all* the family members—the siblings, the children, the in-laws, the close extended family. Your kind words and acknowledgments can make a huge difference in someone's recovery.

(And please do not misunderstand—we realize it is equally difficult to lose a sister as well! All our examples here just happened to revolve around losing brothers.)

Regarding the loss of

~ parents you're close to

~ in-laws

~ extended family

~ close friends

Or death due to

~ miscarriage/stillbirth

~ serving in the military

~ overdose

~ suicide

~ murder

and others we failed to mention, along with even having a wayward child, *first of all*, for those who have walked this road, *please forgive us* for seeming to lump it all together. I know *you* can probably write a book of your experience with the tragedy you have faced!

It's *all* tragic, especially depending on the depth of the relationship. We cannot dismiss someone's loss because of our comprehension, or how we view the dynamic.

To those on the sidelines, open your heart and let someone share their pain with you, because you never know what someone carries in *their* heart.

Here are a few other life-altering losses in our own world.

Our niece had a full-term still-birth delivery. I can't imagine either one of these situations—to lose a baby, or to give birth to one who died in the womb, or shortly after!

Charlie's sister gave birth four months prematurely to a little girl. We got to the house about 2:00 a.m. and paramedics were working frantically to save her. As we walked in, this tiny but fully formed little body lay there on a padded bar stool, and the EMT ever-so-gently continued hand-squeezing air into her lungs with a bulb syringe. She didn't make it. And you know what?! Adding insult to injury, her parents had to suddenly come up with a name for the birth and death certificates! I will never forget this as long as I live. They named her Angel Hope. Without a doubt I *know* Beau and his little cousin Angel Hope are very well acquainted and tight in Heaven!

Our sweet friend Cathy jumped through hoop after hoop—seven years of fervent attempts trying to conceive at the hand of modern medical interventions. She finally received that beautiful phone call confirming her pregnancy and a new little life growing inside. Despite all the valiant efforts and prayers of faith, their joy was short-lived when a few weeks later she lost the baby through miscarriage. The pain and ripping, even several years afterward, has been life-altering for both parents.

BJ and Lisa lost his dad and her father-in-law suddenly a few years ago. They shared with us how hard it was on *both* of them, especially in the months following. People would always reach out to his mother, and sometimes to him, but rarely did anyone ever acknowledge Lisa's pain. She loved her father-in-law so much and was deeply pained by losing him, but it was rare anyone would ever show sympathy to her, the daughter-in-law. She would have to continually hide her grief, which really affects a person's ability to heal. Like having a wound that never gets properly cleaned—it takes ages to close up, and still unexpectedly erupts with some oozing and tenderness even after a long time.

Pat and Sue, who have an ongoing outreach in East Africa, shared with us a saying they have over there where death is very prevalent, given the famine, starvation and untreated-but-curable diseases many regions experience: "If a husband dies, you lose a father. If a mother dies, you lose the family."

Meaning, losing a mother is looked at as almost certain devastation of the family, because of the huge responsibility she carries in the household. We know a family who lost their wife and mother to cancer while the three children were spanning their teen years. How tragic, and how many families have faced a similar plight, with a grieving father left to raise them on his own?! Before his passing, our ninety-year-old uncle would *still* cry over the loss of his mother from breast cancer while he was only sixteen, which greatly pained him throughout his lifetime.

Our nephew's beautiful, early-teenage daughter, Jordy, died from aggressive sarcoma cancer, which has completely ripped his heart out, along with the entire family.

Kelly's teenage daughter took her own life several years ago. Needless to say, it was paralyzing for many years following. The pain is almost incomprehensible that a parent goes through who loses a child to suicide—it's a double blow, for sure. The condemnation that instills afterward is almost beyond comprehension. Kelly had this to say about losing her sweet daughter, Haylie Grace Willard:

> First of all, it is unspeakable pain and shock, when you lose one of your children. I thought the pain would never let up. I laid in bed and cried for two years, but it took a good eight years until something told me to, "Look forward…stop looking back." It was then that I began to get stronger emotionally and physically. Now, all I do is look forward to seeing her again. It makes a huge difference for me. Knowing she's with Jesus has been the greatest comfort of all.

Some are derailed even after losing their parents. They had a *very* close relationship, and were just not ready for them to ever leave this life! We must respect the fact that this is *their* journey and *their* relationship, and maybe not our experience. Honestly, I (Jill) have not shed a tear over either of my parents' passing, but I know it's because our son preceded them in death, which majorly affected both of us in that regard. I loved them dearly, but they both died at an elderly age, and I was relieved *for them* that neither one had to physically suffer any more from their illnesses. And while some have similar experiences, others experience a deep grief and sense of massive loss over the death of their parents, even at an elderly age. *But it's okay!* Even though parents are supposed to precede their children in death, whether or not it happens prematurely, or the adult child was particularly close with their parents, it can be devastating and temporarily paralyzing. We must not judge them.

Be tender with the bereaved. Do your best to offer them love in the form of tenderness, kindness, patience and care—they won't always be this way. We pray you never have to know this kind of pain, but please learn how you can best extend God's compassion to them, being another example of "Jesus with skin on."

CHAPTER NINE

"You Do the Lovin', I'll Do the Fixin'"

*Like apples of gold in settings of silver
is a word spoken at the right time.*

—Proverbs 25:11, AMP

In October 2010, more than one and a half years after our son passed away, we were in Buxton, England, on a Sunday evening, preparing for a conference with Andrew Wommack Ministries that would commence the next day. The team was being seated for dinner at the hotel, and our friend Wendell came into the room, sitting down at our table.

"Did you hear about Clifton and Geri?" he immediately went into it with a very troubled look on his face.

"No. What happened?"

"Their son Kelly was just killed in a tractor accident."

We froze. Our hearts stopped. As I (Jill) sat there while he tried to convey the details he knew, I remember just staring down at the table with a sick feeling flooding my gut. I knew I had to go somewhere fast, so I excused myself from the table and told Charlie I wouldn't be eating.

I quickly made my way to our room, and began crying and sobbing for our dear friends. We knew Kelly—a young man still in his forties, seasoned cowboy and horseman, who patiently let our family ride his horse one afternoon after being with them at his parents' church that weekend.

I knew what they were experiencing—the indescribable, searing pain, the questions, the feeling that your heart will explode inside you.

It wasn't long before Charlie joined me in there, and we both cried and prayed for over an hour. He eventually pulled himself together enough to call Clifton and offer our deepest condolences. Through his own tears, he tried to tell him how sorry we were to hear this, as Clifton began to explain some details of the accident. *So* heart-wrenching.

Through many tears they talked for a short while—maybe ten minutes—and at the end of the conversation, since they pastor a church not far from us, Charlie offered to come the next weekend after returning and minister in their Sunday service so they wouldn't have that burden to "give out," less than two weeks following their son's death.

Immediately, he so gratefully accepted the offer, and we soon said our tearful goodbyes.

After returning home, it was now Sunday and since they were only an hour's drive from us, we drove down that morning.

As we were praying while traveling, Charlie was suddenly overwhelmed with the thought, *What in the world are we doing? There's no way we can do this! I'm just going to get up there and blubber all over the pulpit! What am I going to say?!*

We understood this kind of pain, but were we qualified to say *anything* at this point? We were still so raw and broken ourselves! It's been less than two years! Continuing to pray as we made our way down the hilly two-lane road to this rural, country church, suddenly the Lord spoke to him so clearly, it was almost audible:

Tell the people, You do the lovin' and I'll do the fixin'.

And that was it!

Like a shaft of light from Heaven, the Lord imparted such deep and meaningful words of wisdom, and once again our lives were changed forever.

As we pondered and discussed this revolutionary thought, we knew it would be a key to helping them, along with their members, eventually move forward.

When we arrived at the storefront church building, Clifton and Geri came out to meet us. Honestly, we were very nervous to see them, not knowing what emotional state they would be in. But they were *so* relieved to have this level of support so early in their grief journey, and they greeted us with smiles and warm, grateful hugs.

Be that as it may, it didn't take long for tears to well up and stream down as we unloaded equipment and they began to share more details of the story. All our hearts were hurting so badly, yet we each knew this was an unbelievable, no, more like *unthinkable* event, that the four of us were there at this moment in time, and now with an experience none of us ever wanted to share.

During the service, God's grace and love flowed as we sang songs like *"God is My Refuge," "Beauty for Ashes,"* and *"One With the Lord."* It wasn't long before Charlie put his guitar down and began sharing with them, through tears and tenderness, the word God placed on his heart while driving there earlier.

"…The Lord said, 'You do the lovin', and *I'LL* do the fixin'.'"

After telling them briefly of our own personal experience, he shared how well-meaning people often tried to "fix us," because our state of grief was uncomfortable, and they didn't want to see us suffer. They wanted to help by saying things like:

"Well, thank the Lord, Beau went straight into the arms of Jesus!"

or

"Aren't you so grateful you'll be together again one day?"

or

"Beau wouldn't want you to be sad for him. He's finally free!"

or

"You don't have to grieve anymore. Jesus has carried your grief!"

All these statements are true. But what well-meaning people don't comprehend if they've never walked through it is, these words don't bring comfort at a time like this. These words are for *much* later down the road, if at all.

Like in our own story, from the moment Beau left us, we were fully aware he instantly blasted out of his suffering body straight into the glorious realm of Heaven and met Jesus face-to-face, taking a *long*, *deep* breath without a hint of struggle, and basking in the *joy* of being set free from the prison of that broken body he had lived in the last several months, and especially weeks. We were *thrilled* for him to be so free, so how in the world could we be in the least bit sad, knowing all this?

Because we didn't want him to leave us!

We loved and enjoyed our son so much and wanted to experience years of life with him as he grew in the Lord, got married, had children, and became the man, the prophet, the preacher, and artist he was created to become, to fulfill the God-given purpose he was born for. We wanted him to experience the same miraculous healing to purge his body of this cursed disease like we read in the Gospels and hear about in many others' lives today. We also wanted him to have that healing testimony to share with those battling for their own healing, to encourage their faith.

Alas, our hearts broke into a thousand pieces.

Back in Farmington, we continued sharing with the Coulters' church body the truths of what happens to bereaved people, and how you have to walk in love and patience with them—a *lot* of it! We explained, "Grief has a mind of its own and you just never know when it will hit. So *your* job, as their church family, is to be 'Jesus with skin on.'"

Especially as Christians, we want to "fix" people who are broken, messed up, sick, confused or troubled in any way. With an honest heart of love and concern, we just don't want our friends to be hurting. Many feel they know what to say to remedy the situation at hand, or may feel they have "a word from the Lord" and will boldly say it. Now of course it's good and right to want to help those who are hurting, but you must be very sensitive in the moment. Ecclesiastes 3 reminds us that there is a time for every purpose under Heaven, including a time to weep, a time to laugh, to mourn and to dance; a time to keep silent, *and* a time to speak! But please don't misunderstand—we are not at all against offering something from the Holy Spirit, however one must *really* weigh their words in these raw, extremely tender days, when to say it, and *how* to say it. (More on this to come.)

There are even examples in scripture that demonstrate this same faux pas:

Singing cheerful songs to a person with a heavy heart is like taking someone's coat in cold weather or pouring vinegar in a wound. (Proverbs 25:20 NLT)

And similarly,

A loud and cheerful greeting early in the morning will be taken as a curse! (Proverbs 27:14 NLT)

In other words, we mustn't just assume *our* way of "helping" is what will *actually* help in a situation. But the Holy Spirit can help direct us and our decisions in these times, and we must be sensitive to following His lead.

On this Sunday morning, the Lord gave specific instructions encouraging the congregation to "just love on them" (their pastors). This is what most bereaved people need, for a long time. You do the lovin'. The Lord will, in time, "fix" their broken heart and crushed spirit.

As we read in Psalm 147:3, "*He heals the* brokenhearted *and binds up their wounds.*"

And in Psalm 34:18, "The LORD is close to the brokenhearted and saves those who are crushed in spirit." (NIV)

Jesus is loving and patient with the brokenhearted, and He brings comfort and healing with so much love, just as we should!

CHAPTER TEN

Learning Compassion

We think you ought to know, dear brothers and sisters, about the trouble we went through … We were crushed and overwhelmed beyond our ability to endure, and we thought we would never live through it. … And you are helping us by praying for us.

—2 Corinthians 1:8, 11 NLT

Life can be a good teacher if we will open our hearts to learn.

Jesus was the most compassionate person ever in existence—His life was an actual reflection of Father God's heart! (Hebrews 1:3)

The Bible also tells us, *"We know that for those who love God all things work together for good, for those who are called according to His purpose."* (Romans 8:28 ESV)

Please know, we *do not* embrace the doctrine of God *causing* all things. Yet, we *fully* embrace what it says here, that

He will work all things together for good, for those who love Him, like He did (and continues doing) for us after losing our son. Beau's death was a rip-off from the enemy, but only God can bring good out of something so dark and evil.

Never before have we understood what someone goes through in loss like we do now. How could we have known this level of pain without walking through it ourselves?

There are so many lessons we've learned through this journey. Here are a few:

~ Extreme empathy—*really* understanding someone else's pain or situation, because we've been there.

~ Never to judge someone walking through grief brought on by *any* type of loss.

~ There is *no* timetable to grief, or recovery—everyone is different, and their journey will be as well.

We've also learned there are several different types of loss, each tragic to the one walking through it:

~ The loss of fidelity or trust in your marriage

~ Losing your marriage through divorce

~ Losing your health

~ Losing a body part to illness or an accident

~ Losing a pregnancy

~ Losing trust in someone you love

~ Losing your life's savings

~ Losing your home

~ Losing your job or career

~ Losing a deep relationship

~ Even losing a beloved pet

Loss comes in multiple ways. If you've suffered even one of these blows, think back to how it was when you were in the thick of it—the deep sadness and disillusionment, the confusion, the mind-numbing paralysis, the frustration, or the feeling of helplessness, anger, or disappointment. Now apply this to your friend or relative who has sustained some level of loss, and you can better understand how to walk beside them in their time of difficulty.

In Rick Warren's talk "How To Get Through What You're Going Through," the first time he and Kay were back in the pulpit following their son's suicide, Rick said to his congregation after reading 2 Corinthians 1:3–11:

> I want you to know that we intend for the rest of our lives, to spend the rest of our lives comforting others, with the same comfort that we have been given from God, because of your prayers.[29]

This is exactly where we've landed, as well!

Let's look at a few verses from the passage referenced above:

All praise to God, the Father of our Lord Jesus Christ. God is our merciful Father and the source of all comfort. He comforts us in all our troubles so that we can comfort others. When they are troubled, we will be able to give them the same comfort God has given us ...

We think you ought to know, dear brothers and sisters, about the trouble we went through ... We were crushed and overwhelmed beyond our ability to endure, and we thought we would never live through it. ... And you are helping us by praying for us. Then many people will give thanks because God has graciously answered so many prayers for our safety. (2 Corinthians 1:3–4, 8, 11 NLT)

In these verses, Paul was very transparent about his troubles and sufferings. And because he understood suffering, it is obvious his heart was to be a comfort to the hurting and encourage others to be the same.

This has become a major mandate in our lives now as well. It has become almost second nature to jump in and help someone who is suffering. I pray we all embrace the awesome opportunity to be a balm of love to those in need.

Not everyone in their lifetime will experience an untimely or life-altering loss. For those who haven't, it's hard to relate to many things we are saying. But for those who have suffered this tragedy, we feel a need to defend their grieving hearts and their mourning souls.

Proverbs 31:8–9 confirms this:

Speak up for those who cannot speak for themselves;

ensure justice for those being crushed.

Yes, speak up for the poor and helpless,

and see that they get justice. (NLT)

For many, especially when they first encounter the tragic loss of a loved one, or any earth-shattering event, *they* become the poor and helpless, and cannot speak for themselves, particularly in the beginning. Most times, they're just too broken and paralyzed. We believe the Lord has called all of us to be a voice for them. As He is, *so are we* in this world. (1 John 4:17)

BEING JESUS WITH SKIN ON

Years ago I heard a story of a little boy who was frightened during a storm.

Late one stormy night, a small voice was heard from the bedroom across the hall. "Mommy, I'm scared!"

Mom responds sympathetically "Honey, don't be afraid, I'm right across the hall."

After a short time, with thunder snapping in the distance, the little voice says again, "I'm still scared!"

Mom replies, "You don't need to be afraid. Close your eyes and pray. And remember that Jesus is always with you."

The next time the pause is longer ... but the voice returns, along with a little child standing next to her bed, "Mommy, can I get in bed with you and Daddy?"

As Mom is just about to lose her patience, her little boy catches her eyes and says, "Mommy, I know that Jesus is always with me, but right now I need Jesus with skin on."[30]

This story has spoken volumes to us through the years, and is so applicable in so many instances—*especially* now.

The evening of our son's death, our home was flooded with people—dear friends who just wanted to "be there" with us, and some even traveled from out of state upon hearing the news. Earlier that evening as different ones called to ask if they could come over, Charlie recalls my (Jill's) response being, "Definitely! I need Jesus with skin on!"

Jesus with skin on—this is what we become when we show up like that: Allowing ourselves to be a conduit of God's love to someone so wounded.

It's crucial to be Jesus with skin on to the griever—to be His arms, His hands, His heart to those who are hurting.

Some stayed away that night because it was such a painful loss and they couldn't bear the thought of being with anyone. Understandably, we were *all* so paralyzed at first. But I promise you, as odd as this sounds, being with others who share the same pain can be very affirming and healing. Realizing a community of people were all devastated by the death of our son brought a curious sense of comfort to us, knowing he was so loved, and we weren't alone in our suffering.

One thing the bereaved need is *you*. Just be there for them. Be Jesus with skin on! Unless you've walked this road, you will never fully know the value of having loving friends around, who have no agenda except to offer comfort, companionship, and a shoulder to cry on.

We've met people through the years who say they "just don't go to funerals." My parents taught me long ago, we don't just go for the dead, but we go for the living. We show up to let those closest to the departed know that we care, that we also mourn the loss, our hearts break for *them*, and to let them know they are surrounded with support. A thousand people showed up for our son's first memorial service. Even though we didn't get to speak with each one personally, just standing on stage and seeing the love and support for our family was *so healing* and affirming!

THE LOST ART OF WEEPING WITH THOSE WHO WEEP

As mentioned earlier, Paul told us in Romans 12:15 to weep with those who weep. Through the years, many in our faith communities seem to have almost lost this art of compassion! They are determined to "encourage" the bereaved, sharing Christian principles instead of showing tenderness or endeavoring to be a vessel of God's loving-kindness. In doing this, the well-meaning believer often misses showing mercy and sensitivity. This type of response is actually counterproductive in the healing process of an individual walking through possibly the darkest days of their life. We personally, along with many friends who also walk this road, encountered some of this and even now still experience it. There will be a time for sharing scriptures and insights, but early in the grief journey is not normally optimal.

On the other hand, we can vividly recall those who looked us in the eyes with tears in theirs and hugged us, sometimes saying nothing. You have no idea how weeping with us helped and brought comfort to our souls.

JUST BE THERE

Yet some say, "I'd better not go over because I don't know what to say," or, "I might say the wrong thing." On the contrary, *just being there* can be comforting.

Paul said from prison in Philippians 4:14, *"You've so graciously provided for my essential needs during this season of difficulty"* (TPT). What are "essential needs" for those who just experienced a heartbreaking loss? Basically this, and most importantly: Those you love being there for you.

He also confirmed this here, *"Nevertheless God, who comforts the downcast, comforted us by the coming of Titus."* (2 Corinthians 7:6)

Everyone walks through difficult seasons of one type or another in their lives, and having support from loving individuals during that time is *so valuable* and *never* wasted effort.

We were blown away with the love and support offered to us during the first few months of our bereavement, and especially just afterward. Anything from, "May I come and clean your house?" (or sometimes they just stepped up and *did* it!) to bringing beautiful meals, and one even said, "If you'd like me to paint a room for you, I'm happy to come and do that."

Some very special friends came over and packed up all our Christmas decorations after we left the house, (which they had also set up for us!), and cleaned our entire lower level the day our son passed away, removing all the medical equipment and putting the space back together in a livable manner (I was literally speechless when we returned home and saw this). One dear couple stepped up and *paid* for the mortuary services, and countless people sent in financial gifts over the next several months. *All* of these acts of love and kindness were like fresh air blown into a stale, dark room.

Early on, just being there, or preparing food, to run an errand, take a child to sport practice, cut the grass, put out the trash, wash and fold some laundry, change a light bulb, clean out the fridge from all the old leftovers, or any number of tasks to help out, *this* is being Jesus with skin on.

As we read in Psalm 46:1, we are reminded, *"God is our refuge and our strength, a very present help in trouble."* He is the One who brings supernatural help and peace, no matter what we are walking through. But what a huge blessing to *be* one of the ways through which He does this in others' lives—to be His hands, His feet, and His shoulder to cry on. And remember Matthew 25:40 (NLT), *"And the King will say, 'I tell you the truth, when you did it to one of the least of these My brothers and sisters, you were doing it to Me!'"*

BEARING ONE ANOTHER'S BURDENS

Carry each other's burdens, and in this way you will fulfill the law of Christ. (Galatians 6:2 NIV)

As Jill and I (Charlie) we were just finishing this manuscript, a very dear friend passed away rather unexpectedly. Rich was an incredible Jesus lover who was a great musician with a remarkable intelligence and an insatiable love for the Word of God. Back in the Jesus Movement, we all were great friends including the girl who became his adoring wife, Carla.

After his eight-year battle with cancer, we received the sudden, shocking news Rich was dying. We continued standing with Carla on God's promises for a supernatural miracle healing, yet realizing the possibility that it could go a different way than we were expecting.

Upon receiving Carla's text later that morning, "Rich is in Heaven with Beau now ♥," we were both sucker-punched and hit with unexpected, incredible grief and mourning—not only for the great loss of a longtime friend, but for his wife, his sons, and their families. Over the next several days, it was uncanny how much this affected both of us—we would find ourselves grieving over losing him, and prayed often through hot tears for Carla and the boys.

In the meantime, Carla was swamped with contacting all the family, planning a simple graveside funeral and all the decisions that go along with it, *and* arranging travel and accommodations for almost two dozen family members joining them in LA. But even with all of this, every time she would send a text, there was a lightness in her tone, which to us seemed so unusual, but a huge blessing that she was seemingly not overcome with grief.

However, following the funeral the grief and tears hit me again, but this time it was deeper, uncontrollable, and unusual. I asked the Lord what was going on and what was happening to me. He answered, *Charlie, your tears are intercession for Carla and her boys.*

Immediately I was reminded of the scripture:

Likewise the Spirit also helps in our weaknesses. For we do not know what we should pray for as we ought, but the Spirit Himself makes intercession for us with groanings which cannot be uttered. (Romans 8:26 ESV)

When we finally had the chance to share this experience with Carla after the funeral, she began crying on the phone and now realized *why* she was sleeping so well, waking up refreshed, feeling as if she was being carried and able to function during that potentially overwhelming time. She was so blown away to hear how the burden of grief had been so heavy on *us*, and God's love so beautifully embraced and held her during those tragic days following Rich's passing!

It has been a revelation to us how important it is to yield to the Holy Spirit. We can't manufacture this type of intervention, but we must be willing to "bear one another's burdens," however the Lord would have us do that, and in this way impart to the one grieving, a period of reprieve as they pass through the dreaded "valley of the shadow of death."

Blessed are those who mourn, for they shall be comforted. (Matthew 5:4 NIV)

This act of love *so* fulfills the law of Christ!

Bear one another's burdens, and so fulfill the law of Christ. (Galatians 6:2)

And here it is in the Amplified:

Carry one another's burdens and in this way you will fulfill the requirements of the law of Christ [that is, the law of Christian love]. (AMP)

And one more, from The Passion Translation:

Love empowers us to fulfill the law of the Anointed One as we carry each other's troubles.

We hope you are beginning to learn some things to help in these dark times. Please continue reading to gain more understanding and become that conduit of God's love and grace.

So I give you now a new commandment: Love each other just as much as I have loved you. For when you demonstrate the same love I have for you by loving one another, everyone will know that you're My true followers. (John 13:34–35 TPT)

CHAPTER ELEVEN

"Just Move On"

Those we have held in our arms for a little while,
we hold in our hearts forever.

—Khalil Gibran

A few years into this journey that *no one* wants to traverse, I (Jill) was talking to someone about how the holidays are still so hard. After commenting about how much I miss our son, I was offered some personal advice: "That's when you just have to move on and let it go."

Whoa! Say *what* now?!

Move on? Let it go??

How in the world do you "move on" from watching your beloved adult child, whom you love so much and was a huge part of your life, suffer for nine months and die a gut-wrenching death? And now there is a gaping hole in your heart, filled with dashed dreams and empty hope! Just "move on"?

In all honesty, a general consensus from most who have suffered loss is that this phrase needs to be deleted from the subject of losing close loved ones.

We know what you mean is, "Hurry up and heal so you can get back to normal again!" Unfortunately, it just doesn't happen that way.

Now, please don't misunderstand. I am well aware that in Christ Jesus, old things are passed away and all things have become new (2 Corinthians 5:17). This is referring to our old, sin-laden nature and being born again into our new life in Christ. But the fact is, our past has helped to frame our present and our future. Being born again and redeemed by the sacrificial blood of Jesus removes the sin, guilt and condemnation of our past, but the past experiences in life are still a real part of us and can be used to help others. Our stories are powerful and important!

If we have been set free from a horrible past or healed from a debilitating situation, it makes us *very* thankful to be delivered from that hellish life, and hopefully someone who lives to make a difference for others. He who has been forgiven much, loves much (Luke 7:47). In the same way, if tragedy has struck our lives, it can majorly affect who we are and become in the future. Without shock therapy, a brain transplant, or a miracle from God, it's not likely someone will escape the modifications that will take place in their soul as a result of a life-altering circumstance such as this.

Harriet Schiff, author of *The Bereaved Parent*, put it this way,

> *The reality is that we don't forget, move on, and have closure, but rather we honor, we remember, and incorporate our deceased children and siblings into our lives in a new way. In fact, keeping memories of your loved one alive in your mind and heart is an important part of your healing journey.*[31]

And this is exactly what we did, and it surely was (and still is) a healing *journey*. There is no hasty remedy, nor does it happen in our time frame. It took *years* to get to the place we are today.

Rabbi Grollman so poignantly states,

> *The depth of your sorrow diminishes slowly, and at times imperceptibly. Your recovering is not an act of disloyalty to the one who has died. Nor is it achieved by "forgetting" the past. ... Don't try to destroy a beautiful part of your life because remembering it hurts. As children of today and tomorrow, we are also children of yesterday. The past still travels with us, and what it has been makes us who we are. ... Try to strike that delicate balance between a yesterday that should be remembered and a tomorrow that should be created.*[32]

It's a difficult quandary one finds oneself in when they lose a special person they love. It seems like time following the death speeds by like a runaway train, and suddenly they realize it's been weeks and months since they've held, and much less seen or spoken to their loved one who is now gone. In pondering all this, I (Charlie) took a new look at a scripture I'd known for a while, which seemed to really help me, eventually:

> *Not that I have already attained, or am already perfected; but I press on, that I may lay hold of that for which Christ Jesus has also laid hold of me. Brethren, I do not count myself to have apprehended; but one thing I do, forgetting those things which are behind and reaching forward to those things which are ahead, I press toward the goal for the prize of the upward call of God in Christ Jesus.* (Philippians 3:12–14)

This has been one of the most inspirational scriptures of my life! But now in light of losing our son, how does this fit in?

A mistake often made is that we take scriptures out of their context and try to make them apply to everything. When Paul said in Philippians 3:13 *"Forgetting what things are behind and pressing on to the things ahead,"* he was *not* referring to loved ones who pass away and leaving their memory behind, or our consciousness of them. "Pressing on" means to push through the hard times, pursuing Jesus and the destiny God has for us. It also means to leave your accomplishments behind and don't lean on your own credentials. Paul lists his Hebraic righteousness, the things he had accomplished and the notoriety he had as a Jew; then he countered everything with saying he leaves it all behind and counts it as nothing, compared to knowing Christ (Philippians 3:8).

Just as we all do when we come to Christ, whatever accomplishments we had as non-believers, we lay all at the cross and follow Jesus, looking to Him as the author and finisher of our faith.

We should never mistakenly tell a grieving person to "press on" and leave the memory of their beloved behind. Nor should we tell them to "move on," leaving behind a part of their life that helped make them who they are. It is dysfunctional (and actually impossible) to try and make someone stop thinking about their departed loved ones. If anything, for many of us, remembering our loved ones draws us closer to Jesus, who is caring for our loved ones, and makes our thoughts of Heaven even sweeter.

> For this cause I bow my knees unto the Father of our Lord Jesus Christ, of whom **the whole family in Heaven and Earth** is named. (Ephesians 3:14–15 KJV, emphasis added)

MOVING ON

In looking through our youngest daughter's social posts one day, I came across a TedTalk video by Nora McInerny that she had discovered. I (Jill) watched and found it very affirming for those of us walking through a grief journey. We would like to share a portion of it with you:

> *2014 was a big year for me... It went like this: October 3 I lost my second pregnancy. And then October 8 my dad died of cancer. And then November 25 my husband Aaron died after three years with brain cancer.*
>
> *Now, since 2014, I will tell you that I have remarried a very handsome man named Matthew. We have four children in our blended family... By any measure, life [now] is really, really good. But I have not "moved on."*
>
> *I haven't moved on, and I hate that phrase so much, and I understand why other people do. Because what it says is that, Aaron's life and death and love are just moments that I can leave behind me, and that I probably should. And when I talk about Aaron, I slip so easily into the present tense, and I always thought that made me weird. And then I noticed that everybody does it. And it's not because we are forgetful or in denial, but it's because the people we love who we've lost are still so present in us.*
>
> *These are the experiences that mark us and make us, just as much as the joyful ones, and just as permanently, long after you get your last sympathy card or last hot dish.*
>
> *We don't look at the people around us experiencing life's joys and wonders and tell them to "move on," do we? We don't send a card that's like, "Congratulations*

on your beautiful baby," and then five years later think like, "Another birthday party? Get over it!"

But grief is kind of one of those things like falling in love or having a baby or watching The Wire on HBO—where you don't get it until you get it, or until you do it. And once you do it, once it's your love or your baby, once it's your grief or your front row at the funeral, you get it: You understand that what you're experiencing is not a moment in time, it's not a bone that will reset, but what you've been touched by is something chronic. Something incurable. It's not fatal, but sometimes grief feels like it could be. And if we can't prevent it in one another, what can we do?

We need each other to remember, to help each other remember, that grief is this multi-tasking emotion. That you can and will be sad, and happy; you'll be grieving and able to love in the same year or week, or the same breath. We need to remember that a grieving person is going to laugh again and smile again. If they're lucky, they'll even find love again. But yes, absolutely, they're going to move forward. But that doesn't mean that they've moved on.[33]

This is another poignant depiction of someone's grief journey and the importance of what we say to those at the epicenter. Each of us has our own bent, our individual, unique relationship with the deceased, and no one else can *fully* understand it. One cannot control (and should not judge) how the bereaved should respond and when they should move forward.

Like we mentioned earlier, we were forever changed the day Beau died. That will never go away until we leave this planet, and we will never "move on." *However*, and completely by God's grace and help, we have "moved forward." This is not simply a matter of semantics, but two entirely different paradigms.

We referenced C. S. Lewis earlier. In his book, *A Grief Observed,* he journals losing his wife to cancer after only four years of marriage. Here is more from his journal:

> *Getting over it so soon? But the words are ambiguous. To say the patient is getting over it after an operation for appendicitis is one thing; after he's had his leg off, it is quite another. After that operation either the wounded stump heals or the man dies. If it heals, the fierce, continuous pain will stop. Presently he'll get back his strength and be able to stump about on his wooden leg. He has "got over it."*
>
> *But he will probably have recurrent pains in the stump all his life, and perhaps pretty bad ones; and he will always be a one-legged man. There will be hardly any moment when he forgets it. Bathing, dressing, sitting down and getting up again, even lying in bed, will all be different. His whole way of life will be changed. All sorts of pleasures and activities that he once took for granted will have to be simply written off. Duties too.*

At present I am learning to get about on crutches. Perhaps I shall presently be given a wooden leg. But I shall never be a bi-ped again.[34]

Almost fifteen months after our son died, I (Jill) wrote this. I was "moving forward":

You know, one of the things the Lord showed me shortly after our son left us was this:

The one thing we can still do together (Beau and I) is worship Him (the Lord).

And it was life-altering for me. Eventually.

In the beginning it was hard for me to worship Him because my heart was so wounded and confused. But through the months, this brought me much comfort and hope, knowing my Beau-san is alive and well, just living in a different place, and he is in our future. And we believe when we are worshiping the Father, whether leading a group or privately, Beau is also in the Lord's presence, worshiping Him along with us! Together!

We still miss him terribly. I'm not sure that will ever change. For a long time I was barraged by flashbacks of our journey and all the different ways he suffered physically and emotionally, which about tore my heart out, over and over again. At times I wasn't sure if I could continue living because the pain was so intense. However as time has gone on, the flashbacks are not as frequent or as severe (for the most part), and it seems more feasible that we will be able to carry on with life, just on a different level.

Those of us who've lost close loved ones will carry our "most precious" in our hearts forever. We will never forget them, and in the case of children or siblings, or a close spouse or relationship, we think about them *every day* and several times in a day. Our life has definitely changed because they are gone.

Even those who've lost a spouse they dearly loved and yet found love again, many times still love and miss their departed spouse while being married to another. And that's okay. Once you lose someone who is a part of you, you are never the same. You eventually learn to move forward, but differently than before.

Yes, the "stump" is still there and will never go away (without a supernatural miracle, and they *do* happen!). We laugh, we smile, we enjoy life and can have fun. We dream, we work hard, and some people never know "we have a prosthetic." We have moved forward. But we will always carry in our hearts the memories—the good, bad and difficult—and are learning how to continue living in "a new normal."

So all that to say, we don't "*just move on.*" But, eventually, we are able to *move forward* again.

This is a blog I (Charlie) wrote just two years after Beau passed away, although I never published it. In looking back, even now all these years later, I feel it's important to share. I wrote it with passion because I was hurting so much at the time, but please receive the advice and excuse the rawness it was written from.

It's been two years since Beau died in our home with his family and friends surrounding him, praying for him and believing God that he would be healed. And if he died, we believed he would be raised from the dead.

But he didn't wake up.

Yet some say it's time to "get over it and move on."

We always have to be moving forward, and in fact, someone reminded us at the beginning of this journey that Beau is in our future, so we press on.

David, one of Beau's close friends, encouraged us with this: "The farthest we will ever be from Beau was the day he died. Since then, each day brings us one step closer to Heaven and reuniting with him!"

But to those who say, "You should be over it by now. Let it go!" let me say this:

Beau was twenty-three years old.

I remember when he was conceived and what the Lord spoke to me at that moment regarding his life and calling.

I remember when he was born, when we wrestled, laughed, played sports together, watching him grow and begin his interest in music.

At two years old I watched the gleam in his eyes as he played his brand-new little drum set he got for his birthday.

We hunted together, skied together, pitched baseballs, threw footballs, kicked soccer balls, played ice hockey, basketball, baseball, football, paint guns. I remember when he got his first car, his first high school dance and his graduation. I remember how much I enjoyed his incredible talent in music with writing, producing and singing. Watched him perform on drums, sing in boy bands, vocal bands in high school and then in all his R&B bands.

Oh yeah! What about his dancing days! Wow! What a dancer the little Timberlake lookalike was, and he didn't have a shy bone in his body. Weddings, parties, you name it, he was in the middle of the floor doing it all. A friend who went to high school with him told me Beau would sing at his locker at the top of his lungs every day and didn't care who was listening.

And what a comedian! He would've been great at standup! No one made me laugh like he did. And I really miss that.

He was also my style consultant, always keeping me current! Talk about an eye for fashion—the guy could've gone so many different directions in life with all his different giftings and talents.

On top of all that, he was a very deep, mature, spiritual young man. Maybe he didn't always walk the straight-and-narrow (who does?), but man he had depth and always loved God and God's Word. He would always help a friend in need and have a positive word to share with anyone needing encouragement. He had a gift of wisdom and all his friends knew it. During his health crisis, his relationship with God became greater and more meaningful than ever.

I could go on and on about how incredible of a guy he was, and what a special gift to have him as a son for twenty-three years here on Earth.

So let me just say to those who say I should be over it by now—you just don't know what it's like to lose a son you are so closely connected to!

How about this—maybe since I have twenty-three years of amazing memories, then maybe, just maybe after twenty-three years without him here with us, you can tell me I should be over it by then. How's that for fairness??? But by that time, all the memories we created for twenty-three years will be even deeper and more meaningful, so even then, it's probably not a fair wager.

The truth is, we will NEVER be "over it."

He was our son and we will carry him in our hearts every day of our lives on this side of Heaven. We will talk about him, laugh about him and cry about him for the rest of our lives. This is what life has dealt us and we will survive, and by God's grace, even thrive as a result of this disappointment and pain.

We will become better and not bitter.

We will carry on with the blow that has been dealt to us, but more importantly we will live the life God has for us!

We will not be defeated, as Paul said in 2 Corinthians 4:8–9 (NIV):

We are hard-pressed on every side, but not crushed; perplexed, but not in despair; persecuted, but not abandoned; struck down, but not destroyed.

And check this out in The Passion Translation,

Though we experience every kind of pressure, we're not crushed. At times we don't know what to do, but quitting is not an option. We are persecuted by others, but God has not forsaken us. We may be knocked down, but not out.

We will make it and we will be fine. In fact I believe that we will be better than before. We will take this pain and the suffering we have and are enduring, and we will allow it to form great character, love, compassion, patience and empathy in our lives.

We are and will become all God wants us to be.

We will take this pain and turn it into a purpose and become a greater blessing to the world.

So, don't judge us! You live your life with God without judging me and I will live my life with God without judging you. Don't try to correct or counsel me unless I ask. Let God be the fixer and you just be the lover.

God can handle this in our lives.

Not at all to say we don't need each other—In truth, we need you more than ever! And like Jill said, "we need Jesus with skin on"—and that's you!

We don't need Job's friends telling us when and how to get over this and try to judge why it happened.

As the song says, "All you need is love," and the love of God will get us through, heal the broken places, comfort us who mourn and bind up our wounds.

A bruised reed he will not break, and a smoldering wick he will not snuff out. (Isaiah 42:3 NIV)

We love all our friends and need you now more than ever, but please don't try to fix us and judge our recovery. Leave that part to God, but please continue to be a good friend—one who can talk and remember and

*understand with compassion, one who can be real and
yet make us laugh when it's appropriate, and also cry
with us when we need to cry. Now that's a real friend.*

*Rejoice with those who rejoice, and weep with those
who weep.* (Romans 12:15)

I realize if you have not been through something like this, it
is hard to understand what it's like. That's the whole reason we
wrote this book and why you're reading it—so you can learn
to have more compassion and understanding to help your
grieving friend or loved one. We must let the bereaved walk
through their grief journey, while we keep loving and just being
there for them.

I hope these thoughts don't come across too harsh, but
I just had to address it, because too many are not being
sensitive to the pain others are going through. As the Bible
says, *"And now abide faith, hope, and love, … but the greatest
of these is love."* (1 Corinthians 13:13)

Just like Jesus did, may love and compassion be the
foremost anchor in our hearts, allowing grievers to move
forward as they are ready.

CHAPTER TWELVE

Stories and Situations

*Jesus used many similar stories and illustrations
to teach the people as much as they could understand.*

—Mark 4:33, NLT

In the face of certain losses, those on the outside
sometimes do not esteem certain situations as tragic as others.
Despite this, after what we've walked through, we've learned to
never judge someone while they are grieving.

Please keep in mind: The Lord deeply cares for the hurting.

*When He saw the vast crowds of people, Jesus' heart
was deeply moved with compassion, because they
seemed weary and helpless, like wandering sheep
without a shepherd.* (Matthew 9:36 TPT)

As the saying goes, "Don't judge a man until you have
walked a mile in his shoes." However, instead of judging,
show them some love. We should never think someone is less

spiritual because they are grieving hard over losing their loved one, or more spiritual because they are seemingly unemotional regarding a loss.

Instead, let's be like the Lord, Who doesn't condemn us but cares about our broken souls: *"…for you have seen my troubles, and you care about the anguish of my soul."* (Psalm 31:7 NLT)

HOW DO PEOPLE CARRY ON?

Where we lived in the early 1980s, there was an awesome, godly, affluent family who appeared as the epitome of a Christ-centered home, with four strapping boys, all of them the picture of godliness—handsome, friendly, respectful, and loving. We met this family and became somewhat acquainted with the boys, as one was a budding musician. And like everyone else, we had really come to admire them—a great example we all aspired to be like.

Their family owned a plane and the two older boys had learned to fly and gotten their pilot's licenses. They would often take trips up to the high country and back to the valley on weekends. But late one sunny Sunday afternoon, as three of the boys were flying back home, somehow they came in too low and flew into some power lines, causing the plane to crash and killing all three of them.

I remember attending the funeral—we were asked to sing at the service our song, "One with the Lord." The chorus begins, "O what a joy it is to be one with the Lord." I recall thinking during the service, *How can the parents be smiling and sharing so calmly about their sons… **three** of their **children**, who were just tragically killed?!*

Since that time I've come to believe, during this period following a loss, many times it seems the Lord gently and temporarily anesthetizes our souls, giving us special grace so we can carry on crucial functions like breathing, eating, and sleeping while we deal with the immediate needs of the situation—notifying family and friends, preparing for the memorial service, burial, dealing with the authorities, emergency services, and not to mention any end-of-life documentation (life insurance and the like) to be handled. This was definitely our own experience.

As time went on, after we moved away from the region, we would continue asking about the family. At first they hung in there, staying involved in the church where they attended as before.

Our future trips there weren't as frequent and we eventually lost touch with the family. I've thought of them through the years and recalled this tragedy many times. And up until our own loss, I would think, *I'm sure they're over it by now and moving on.*

But now, over fourteen years since our own son died, and knowing the ripping, the crushing, the memories, the missing that never leaves, I know this family has *never* been the same! How could they be?! *Three* children died all at the same time and their fourth and youngest is now their *only* remaining son. Who could survive that? I'm sure they have learned to carry on, but the amputation and reconstruction of their family has changed them forever, inside and out.

During those times, we're just thankful for God's strength to carry them, His grace to keep them going, one breath at a time, and mostly for Heaven, that they'll all be together again one day. But that one day can seem like a L-O-N-G time away, especially in the aftermath of such a horrendous tragedy!

SOMETIMES IT TAKES A MIRACLE

On another note, *only* God's incredible, unfathomable grace can heal the heart of one whose accidental actions led to the cutting short of their own loved ones' lives.

Years ago our friend Carol was driving and fell asleep at the wheel. As a result, her husband and one of their daughters lost their lives that day. She and two other daughters survived the accident physically, but the duress and trauma almost killed her in the aftermath.

However, she has a miraculous story of a supernatural healing, which took place years later, in which the heavy blanket of grief, guilt, and condemnation was completely removed from her soul, and she was instantly freed from this torturing darkness.

We must always give place for the power of God to work in a person's life, bringing deliverance and freedom. But until this happens, most people will likely need the hands, heart and feet of Jesus (i.e. *ours*) to help them reach a more functional and healthier place in their lives. (You can read Carol's entire story in her husband's book, *Living With No Regrets*, www .GregFritzMinistries.com.)

THE UNTHINKABLE HAPPENS

We have some dear friends in Northern Ireland whose young son was killed while riding his bike and hit by a car. *So* tragic. This was a couple of years before our loss, and I just couldn't even comprehend at the time the pain they must be living in.

We were already scheduled to be in the UK just a short time later, and made a special trip over from England simply to spend a little time just being there. I was so nervous to see them, especially our initial encounter. I just didn't know whether to keep a stiff upper lip and act like all was good, to be somber and tearful (which I was constantly fighting back), or just follow their lead, which is what we chose.

When they arrived at our hotel to pick us up, we were astonished at their demeanor! They were so happy to see us, and God's amazing grace was all over them. They were joyful and practically glowing with His peace and love.

Shorty after settling into their car en route to a restaurant, we expressed our extreme sorrow and deepest sympathies to them, and how broken we were hearing the news of the accident and Zachary's death.

Humbly yet with a somber joy mixed with some tears, they shared with us over the course of the evening all they experienced, and the beautiful assurance of Jesus now holding their dear son safely in His big arms. Although it was painful to relive the accident and holding his son's lifeless body while awaiting emergency services, it was beautiful to experience God's bountiful grace surrounding and carrying our dear friends during this tender time.

CAN THE MARRIAGE SURVIVE?

We once met a family whose world was tragically turned upside down through loss.

One afternoon their son was riding in a car with other friends, and they were driving crazy through a large county park with lots of curvy, hilly roads, as teenage boys do. After several thrills and frills, the driver lost control and slammed the car into a tree. Everyone walked away from the scene except for one fatality—the son of our friends.

Fast-forward several years—this couple is no longer together. The pain of the loss destroyed their family. We *so* understand this now. The aftermath is just so hard!

The evening of our son's memorial service, a pastor friend pulled us aside and warned us about how hard the enemy of our souls will try and use this loss to place a wedge between us, for the purpose of destroying our marriage. Since this time we've heard many different statistics quoted as to "the divorce rate following loss of child," and most who quote these stats say it is scary high.

Our own research into these figures shows the number is *all over the map*, even showing many couples grow *closer* as a result of their tragedy, which thankfully is our story![35] We took this to heart and became very keen to guard our relationship from the beginning of this journey. So suffice it to say, anything is possible in the aftermath.

It is very important to be sensitive in how any grieving couple is making it through the pain of their loss. Although it was "their" child who passed away, individually they both lost a child—two broken hearts, ripped open and bleeding profusely. Without special support or guidance, especially early on, they could so easily become a statistic.

It could be they secretly blame the other for the outcome and are beginning to harbor bitterness, which then is compounded by their own grief.

They may show up at church smiling, and when you ask how they are, they may say, "Oh fine," or "I'm okay," just to skirt the pain of having to talk about it *again*, along with the issues they are having between each other.

Maybe one doesn't feel comfortable grieving around their spouse, so they are constantly stuffing their emotions, which then builds up like an underground geyser (which will *always* make its way to the surface one way or another, and usually when it's *very* inconvenient)!

Your mourning friends may need a little help learning how to be sensitive to the other one's grief journey. So consider this: if you're the friend of someone grieving, take your friend out to lunch and just listen. He or she may reveal hints that they are struggling in their relationship, and when you've learned some tools on helping the grieving, perhaps you'll be equipped to impart some wisdom. Delicately inquire if you can help in any way. You can tell them some of the things we did (below), including having extreme compassion for each other, recognizing that they both, individually, lost a child.

HOW WE COMMUNICATED

The last thing Charlie and I wanted to do was cause each other more pain, pouring even more salt into the cavernous wound. So here is one of the ways we navigated through, especially early on:

We discovered in our immediate family how we all grieved differently—what one person loved brought heartache to another. For example one thing I (Jill) loved, along with our daughter Camille, was looking at photos of Beau growing up and his young adult life, but this was so painful for Charlie and our daughter Cherrie. So we did our best to respect each other in this, and I kept my photo gazing to my private time. This can be frustrating, but as we mentioned before, it's very important to know your family's individual "pain thresholds," as well as your own.

We found each day was different, and learned we had to establish ground rules early on to not offend each other. For instance, some days would find one of us being bitey and short fused toward the other and having a particularly difficult day emotionally. Initially we wouldn't always comprehend what was going on inside, but finally came to recognize we were grieving! *It was grief!!* Since we were both in this together, we would communicate our struggle, ask forgiveness and to *please* not take it personally—it was a "grief attack," and that we just needed a little more space and grace that day.

This act of love became *huge* in our recovery and keeping the enemy from getting a wedge between us.

Thankfully, those days are *much* fewer and much further between; however we *still* share with each other when difficult days come, and we know this has been a major player in helping us heal, keeping us together and our relationship strong.

> *I forgive whatever needs to be forgiven … so that satan will not outsmart us. For we are familiar with his evil schemes.* (2 Corinthians 2:10–11 NLT)

We were *derailed* after losing our son. It took me (Jill) over ten years to even be ready to move forward in ministry again, and *only* with God's help and grace. He carried us and walked with us all along the way as we ever-so-slowly recovered to this point. And in His perfect patience, He waited until we were ready to move forward, repairing our broken places and strengthening our foundation, enabling us to step into new phases of our lives and ministry.

So please always keep in mind: Someone who walks through devastating loss is never the same! Even ten, twenty, or more years later. What they've walked through has shaped them into who they've become. Even if you feel you would walk through a similar situation differently, you must not expect others to do it like you would.

Be prepared to work with them as someone who has gone through an extremely difficult, damaging situation. Your labor in the Lord will not be in vain, and you will become a safe harbor in their healing journey and their survival.

AND THEN THERE'S "THE HOLIDAYS"...

For many walking the grief road, "The Most Wonderful Time" unfortunately really becomes more like, "The Most Dreaded Time of the Year," (at least for a while)!

At the time of this writing, it has been more than fourteen years since our son passed away, and if anything, we miss him even more now! It's not like we make an effort to memorialize this time, but it just happens. Knowing he died just three weeks after Christmas and how ill he was during his last Christmas here on Earth, all of it makes this entire season pretty tender—and at first, it was really rather bitter.

Honestly, I (Jill) just wanted to skip it all together for a few years, but for the sake of others, we would schlep out the big pre-lit tree and place a few things around the house, just to avoid looking Scrooge-ish. And when our daughters and then eventually our grandchildren would come to visit, we tried to make it a little more welcoming than what we really felt inside.

As years passed, after we moved to Florida to live near our family, I would secretly "go underground" in my soul and pretty much only do it for the grandkids. I hated this, but it's all I could do. So at the eleventh Christmas after Beau's passing, hoping for a new "spark," I even bought all new decorations for our tree, making it very kid-centric instead of traditional. It was fun and cute (thanks Pinterest and Michael's!), but the "joy" was short-lived, for even approaching the twelfth year, it was still really hard. I could only bring myself to keep everything very minimal the next year.

Every Christmas that comes is one more without him, and each year, pulling out all the sentimental decor, his stocking, ornaments and photos, always stirs up a painful emotion, not to mention the memories.

Oh, those memories…

Maybe I just need to box up "his" things separately and not pack them with the rest of it, and stuff them away like I've had to do with most of his physical items that we still have—just keep stuffing it away, along with the recurring memories and emotions. Someday it may not be so painful, but at least during these years, a heaviness still lingers.

As we mentioned earlier, one man of God, who lost two daughters at different times from completely different circumstances, shared a very rich and extremely helpful nugget with us early on. He said to Charlie in a text, "Be kind to yourself." These four words gave us permission to not force ourselves into uncomfortable situations as we walked through difficult seasons of our recovery. In reaching these yearly events—birthdays, anniversaries of their passing (or a divorce), wedding anniversaries and others—we the grievers just have to do what we can to get through them. Honestly, I have brought and still bring it to our loving Father in prayer, and even now His grace will come to carry me through a moment so I can get past it to the next one.

Early on, when I would hear the song, "It's the Most Wonderful Time of the Year," it used to make me recoil, want to curl up in bed and pull the covers over my head. Now I just roll my eyes (even if only on the inside) and try to do what I have to so I can push through. It may not always be this way, but only time, and continuing to receive God's beautiful outpouring of grace, will tell.

CHAPTER THIRTEEN

Guidelines to Help Your Grieving Friend

WHAT BRINGS COMFORT AND WHAT DOESN'T

It is believed Theodore Roosevelt said, "Nobody cares how much you know, until they know how much you care."[36]

We've said it before but we must say it again: as you are helping someone who is grieving, please be sensitive, and remember there *is* a timing involved for things we may want to say to those who are hurting. And, there may be some things we should just never say.

Angela Miller, a bereaved parent and author of *You Are the Mother of all Mothers*, said: "My child died, I don't need your advice. All I need is for you to gently close your mouth, open wide your heart and walk with me until I can see color again."[37]

A good example of this in the Bible is from Job's story.

When three of Job's friends heard of the tragedy he had suffered, they got together and traveled from their homes to comfort and console him. Their names were

Eliphaz, Bildad and Zophar. When they saw Job from a distance, they scarcely recognized him. Wailing loudly, they tore their robes and threw dust into the air over their heads to show their grief. Then they sat on the ground with him for seven days and nights.

This next verse is a very meaningful statement:

No one said a word to Job, for they saw that his suffering was too great for words. (Job 2:11–13 NLT)

In reality, most unexpected losses should leave us speechless. There are just no words for some situations but there is *plenty* of room for LOVE! The scripture says that love covers a multitude of sins, and the Lord spoke to me that love also covers a multitude of grief!

Notice however, after Job's friends sat in silence for seven days, they made the all-too-familiar human mistake, giving wrong advice and all their ideas as to why this happened to Job. His friends started well, but as the Lord pointed out, they ended poorly, making misguided statements regarding their observations:

After the Lord had finished speaking to Job, he said to Eliphaz the Temanite: "I am angry with you and your two friends, for you have not spoken accurately about me, as my servant Job has." (Job 42:7 NLT)

Yikes!

As one preacher said rather brashly, "Just show up and shut up." Yes, it's a little harsh, but no doubt is something to consider.

Solomon wisely wrote:

[There is] *a time to be silent and a time to speak.* (Ecclesiastes 3:7 NIV)

And this:

The words of the reckless pierce like swords, but the tongue of the wise brings healing. (Proverbs 12:18 NIV)

Some might say that grieving people are self-centered. Maybe they are, but not selfish. *Their* world has just collapsed around them. *Their* heart is completely broken. *Their* life has just been turned upside down and *they* are at a loss on what to do.

One author said it this way: "The pronouns of grief: I—Me—My. Do not feel ashamed at constantly referring to yourself."[38]

Here are some guidelines a friend can do that will help the griever in their time of mourning.

THE POWER OF BEING PRESENT

We must be fully present with the bereaved for the compassion of the Lord to flow unhindered from our hearts to theirs.

As we read above, when incomprehensible tragedy struck his life, Job's friends showed up and just sat with him for seven days. This became the Jewish tradition of "sitting shiva." *Shiva* is Hebrew for the number seven, and is standard practice to this day, to come over and "just be there" with those newly bereft, traditionally for seven days. They bring food, offer comfort, cry together, sit and chat, and without realizing it they are being Jesus with skin on!

Never underestimate the power of simply being there. When someone is hurting and enduring extreme hardship, we can become timid and insecure toward them. We wonder, *Should I go visit? Will I be a bother? What will I say?* But when you are the one hurting, you need safe friends to talk to. Yes, God will be there with His presence and His love, but He uses *us*. We are His hands, we are His feet, we are His arms that can hug someone when they are hurting.

People need your presence, not your solutions or theology. There is a time and place for everything, and when someone is grieving deeply, being there for them is huge. Listen and let them bleed as they share their broken hearts and memories. This is part of the process and they need listeners, not instructors. We are sometimes quick to pull out our scriptures and counsel, but then we miss the greater things like love and compassion. Remember, the greatest of these is love.

The apostle Paul put it like this:

When we came into Macedonia, we had no rest, but we were harassed at every turn—conflicts on the outside,

*fears within. But God, who comforts the downcast,
comforted us **by the coming of Titus** and not only by
his coming but also by the comfort you had given him.
He told us about your longing for me, your deep sorrow,
your ardent concern for me, so that my joy was greater
than ever.* (2 Corinthians 7:5–7 NIV)

Notice how the God of All Comfort comforted Paul by
Titus' visit, *and God will use you also*, as you simply show up
and are present.

Along with this, Paul was comforted hearing from Titus
that his friends were also thinking about him, as Titus brought
condolences from Paul's other friends. It does help to hear
how others are praying, standing with, and hurting with you. It
really means a lot! If you're not able to physically be there with
them, definitely text, email or call them, maybe even weekly or
monthly, depending upon your relationship.

Even a card sent in the mail, a nice food basket, and
sometimes flowers or plants bring a "virtual hug" to your
grieving friend. A word of caution—some people become
overwhelmed with flowers, as they take up space and need
care, so consider each situation before acting and ask the Lord,
"What would be the best way to help in *this* situation?" The
mother of some very close friends passed away in their home,
and the entire family was there constantly. We prayed about
how we could be a support, and ended up having platters
of food delivered from a local big box store via a personal
delivery service. This turned out to be a major blessing for our
friends and their family walking through this new bereavement!

It was a way of virtually being there to help them across the miles, without physically being there.

BE A GOOD LISTENER

Please do not take the brevity of this section as being any less important, as this lesson is HUGE in being an effective helper to those in mourning.

It's very important to let those who are grieving express themselves. They just need a safe person to talk with about what happened, how special their loved one was, and "what now?" And possibly many times over.

A friend texted after we spent time with him and his wife not long after their son passed away:

"Thanks Charlie—we so enjoyed being together. And thank you for listening."

Sometimes, all they need is a listening ear.

We also learned a very important pitfall: when gathering with your newly bereaved friend, it's important to focus on THEM, and not on our own similar story. Even though some of us can personally identify with loss because we've been there, it's not always the best time to let them know how much *we* understand. As an example, "O I know what you mean. I felt the same way," and then one goes off telling their own experience instead of L-I-S-T-E-N-I-N-G. This natural tendency here is to try and encourage a griever by talking about what happened to *us* and how God helped *us*; however it isn't always the right thing to do at that time. But it *is* time for us to listen and to affirm them.

One blogger said it this way:

We may have experienced very real, similar, painful and difficult things. But in a moment when someone is grieving their own personal loss, one that is theirs and theirs alone, what becomes important is not what WE have gone through. It is being able to focus and be present with what they have gone through.

By remembering how WE felt, we actually become less able to hear honestly how they are feeling. Our brains are now busy thinking about the connections to our own story, or about what we are going to say next to tell them about us.[39]

Let's learn how to be sensitive to people's pain. Hold back from saying the obvious and take time to pray, even under your breath about what you might say. Remember the scripture says to *"be slow to speak and quick to listen"* (James 1:19), and as some have even said, "God gave us two ears and one mouth, so we should be listening much more than talking."

BE A SAFE FRIEND

We encountered so many different kinds of responses after our son passed away. Some people were *so* compassionate and would share and express their own deep grief and sorrow over his death. Others found it hard to say the right thing, or just shallowly recited the typical, standard responses; and still others did not acknowledge our loss at all. Some wanted to "encourage" us by saying things that were not clearly thought through, and secretly caused us to recoil in self-preservation.

During this season, we came to the point of classifying some people we know as "safe friends." Safe Friends were the ones we would literally feel safe with and could let down our protective shield for a while. They're the ones who listened with caring hearts. They let us talk about Beau, about the journey, about our broken hearts, anger and frustration without judging. They were *just there* for us. They didn't try to "fix us" and they weren't afraid to shed tears *with* us. They showed genuine compassion for our pain, and hurt along with us.

Will you be that kind of friend—a Safe Friend who can listen with true compassion and no judgment? I know it can be hard, especially if you really don't understand what they're going through. But please try—try to understand and just be a friend they can lean on and feel free to express themselves, without trying to make it all better. This is so needed in the body of Christ and in the world.

The morning of our son's passing, one sincere person sat with me and just smiled as I expressed my frustration and pain. I thought it was odd, her smiling as I "bled." Her lighthearted expression said to me, "Dear One, if you would just look to see what Beau is experiencing right now, you wouldn't cry, but rejoice." I understood my friend's heart, but what she and many don't understand in these situations is, this did not help.

I remember two years after Beau passed, we were in England leading worship at a large conference, yet we were still hurting so deeply inside. Some dear pastor friends asked us to lunch. We took the chance and accepted their invitation, not knowing for sure if we would feel safe. Thankfully we were seated in a semi-secluded area in the restaurant, and didn't realize what a blessing that would be!

Charlie remembers it this way:

After we ordered, John looked at me with eyes full of Jesus' love, and with great compassion asked how I was "really doing." At that point, the dam burst wide open and I could not stop the torrent of tears as I sat there sobbing across the table.

With tears in their own eyes, John and Susan sat quietly as they just listened to my pain without judgment, and assured me they would stand with us, and even defend us through the whole healing journey.

Someone might say, "What do you mean, 'defend you'?"

Well, when you are recovering from a debilitating situation in your life, you can bet there are people talking about you and deciphering all you've done and are doing which are right and wrong. And, like we've mentioned, they are expecting you to "move on." This is why it is crucial, as we pointed out earlier, to defend and speak up for those who cannot speak for themselves.

AFFIRM AND ACKNOWLEDGE

Even though they may not realize it, a bereaved person very much needs someone to recognize their pain and for it to be acknowledged. If you are able, even briefly, take it upon yourself to try and be a gentle heart, a listening ear, a loving advocate.

Even though you may not completely understand, reach out and affirm them. At the least, let them know you realize their situation is extremely painful, heart-wrenching, and that you can't imagine being in their place. These words alone can lift up the one suffering, allowing them to come up for a much-needed breath of fresh air and can make an immense difference in their recovery.

> *The right word spoken at the right time is as beautiful as gold apples in a silver bowl.* (Proverbs 25:11 NCV)

The first time you are actually with the bereaved after their world has turned upside down, without question, acknowledge their loss. *Please* do not be silent about what has happened— say something. It may make them cry, but these are good tears, cleansing tears. Even if you sent communication following the passing (flowers, a card), and even if it's been a while a while since the death, do not treat it like the elephant in the room, not wanting to say the obvious. I promise you, *they gain affirmation through acknowledgment.*

Oddly enough, when you do *not* say something, it can be *very* hurtful to the one surviving. So not only does the griever have to work through the pain of their loss, they now wonder, *I thought this friend knew what happened.* Or, *Does she even care how much I'm still hurting? I just want to hear his name mentioned again.* Or, *Please bring it up!* But some people are just uncomfortable saying something, being unsure of the right thing to say, or if anything should even be said.

I like how author T. J. Wray shares a similar situation,

Most people don't mean to be insensitive; they just operate under the false notion that bringing up our loss only causes us more grief. I'm able to understand such logic now; but in early grief, it's hurtful when people avoid mentioning something that quite literally occupies nearly every thought. Grief, especially at the beginning, is beneath the surface of nearly everything we say and do. As my sister Robin once said, "I don't know why people feel like they can't mention it, since it's all I think about, anyway."[40]

Six months after Beau passed, we were so blessed with our first grandchild—a baby boy. Our daughter and then son-in-law honored our departed son by giving him the middle name BeauCharles (Charles is Beau's middle name). We were so very blessed by that acknowledgment and still are to this day. What a special blessing it was to see our beautiful baby-boy grandson come into the world, even though we were still hurting so badly from *our* baby boy's departure.

As it does, news got around to all our friends about the birth of our new grandson. Unfortunately what also got around is, as we heard through the months following, several had said, "Well, that will make everything ok now! Charlie and Jill have a grand*son* so they will not be hurting as much anymore. This will really help in their healing process!" Noble thought, but unfortunately it's not *quite* how this works.

In fact, it became a bit irritating when people would approach us within the months after Beau passed, and do nothing but talk and ask about our new grandson, without mentioning a word about Beau and the pain we were experiencing. It came across to us as if they were trying to distract us from thinking about Beau and open our minds to realize the blessing of having a grandson (and now, grand*sons*). Like we said, it just does not work this way.

When you lose a loved one you are so close to, you never stop thinking about them, especially in the beginning. Of course, we were blessed and overjoyed that God gave us a beautiful grandson, and he is *so* special. *But* neither he nor anyone can take the place of our own son, and he is not supposed to.

When a beautiful new season opens up in the life of someone who has experienced deep loss, please do not try and distract them from their own pain. Again, acknowledge the loss, and let *them* tell you what a blessing the new development in their life may be. In reality, for our entire family, our new baby was a precious "distraction" and a healing balm to our broken hearts, but not by *any* sense was he a quick fix for our wounded souls.

WHAT NOT TO SAY

Rabbi Grollman also addresses the subject of unsolicited advice:

Everyone knows what is best for you. People offer words of consolation:

"I know just how you feel".

You want to scream:

No You Don't! How can you possibly know what I'm going through?

"You are doing so well."

Do you know how I feel when you leave?

"Your loved one lived to a ripe old age."

At any age, death is a robber.

"Others have lived through it."

I'm not concerned about others. At this moment I'm concerned about myself.

"It's God's will."

Then this vindictive and vengeful God must be my enemy.[41]

Before I learned better, I (Jill) would say some very shallow (a.k.a. S-T-U-P-I-D) things to the grieving. Here are a couple of embarassing examples.

A disabled Bible college student died in his sleep late into the school year, a couple of months before graduation. I said to other classmates, "Mike wanted to beat everyone else by graduating early!" There were a few "courtesy chuckles," but how insensitive of me, and hopefully there were no family or close friends within earshot!

Another friend, always a jokester, passed away in his late fifties. When we arrived at the funeral and saw his wife just before the service started, I lightheartedly blurted out,

"Can you believe him?! He just *had* to beat you and the rest of us to Heaven!"

She flashed a half smile, along with the couple walking her into the chapel, and then I realized what I said was *so* inappropriate! Do you ever wish you could rewind the words that just came out of your mouth?! I wanted to crawl into a hole! There is a time for weeping and a time for laughter. This was *not* the time for laughter!

Here are a few more things that are best to *not* say to the one suffering loss, *especially* early on:

~ "Don't cry. *Rejoice!* Nehemiah 8:10 says 'The joy of
   the Lord is your strength!'"

  • Early on is just not the time for this.

~ "Thank God you'll see them again."

- Honestly, Christians know this, but in their time of mourning, generally this is not comforting.

~ "Well, praise the Lord, they're in Heaven!"

- They know that too. But they're not here—we want them here!

~ "You doing good?"

- Uhh, no! How do you expect me to be when my child (or spouse or sibling or any close loved one) recently died?!

~ "Well you know they would want you to…

   * be happy for them."

   * carry on with your life."

   * be strong for the rest of the family."

   * rejoice that they're not suffering any more."

- Although this is true and honorable, it doesn't help me deal with the fact that they're gone forever. Yes, they've got it made now, but my life just fell apart.

~ "Oh, I know how you feel. My dog was like a child to me, and he died last week."

- Well, it's just not quite the same. We're so sorry for your pain, and we know this has been

SO HARD on you, but please don't say this to someone who just lost their human.

~ "My ninety-year-old dad just passed. Like you, I've also been in deep mourning."

- Again, not to dismiss your grief which we realize is difficult, but please consider the circumstances before vocally comparing this kind of loss with a more untimely death.

In reality, many of these statements are true and can be a blessing for them to ponder later on down the road when the initial shock wanes and life begins normalizing a little, but do not expect that early on, and PLEASE do not say it! Many well-intended thoughts *we* have to help or rebuild them just need to wait, as we allow the Lord to speak to the bereaved in *His* own timing, when He knows they're ready.

We don't need to have all the answers. We just need to have a tender heart of love to help soften the blow of the loss.

But we'd like to address a problematic statement, often said in some Christian circles, which many times becomes troublesome to the griever:

"You need to rebuke that spirit of grief."

Is there *really* a spirit of grief, in the sense of it being an evil spirit? We don't see that in scripture. Like we pointed out before, we certainly do not grieve like an unbeliever who has no hope (1 Thessalonians 4:13). Yet throughout the scriptures, we see where godly men and women deeply grieved over their losses, and it certainly wasn't an evil spirit.

God created us to grieve over loss, to help process what has happened to us. In a way it's like anesthesia for our soul to help us cope, or like a steam vent on a pressure cooker. Again, Jesus Himself said, *"Blessed are those who mourn, for they shall be comforted."* (Matthew 5:4)

We *must* mourn, or we will implode (and sometimes *explode!*). Like a kettle of water boiling, at some point you have to release that pressure or it starts screaming! But when we *do* release it, we often find at least a momentary relief, and our emotions temporarily become more bearable.

Like we keep saying, there is a time and place for everything. Even though some continue to be sorrowful years later when thinking about and missing their loved one who is gone, it does not mean they will be forever dysfunctional. Jesus does heal broken hearts, and at some point—and no one knows when that is—they should be able to breathe again, dream again and move forward with the life God has planned for them, on *this* side of Heaven, but they will never be the same again.

We just crossed the fourteen-year anniversary of our son's passing. Fourteen years! One may think it would be a "fairly normal day" by now, kind of like 9/11 has become for most people—at least those who didn't lose loved ones then. As we approach "Beau's Day" each year, the day he entered into Life as we can only imagine, we always allow time away from work and normal life to ponder, gather with our daughers, remember, and reflect. This past year, we honestly were not expecting a stir of emotions—after all, it's been fourteen years! But as we've shared, grief comes when you really don't expect it, and sure enough, it didn't "disappoint" (figuratively speaking!). Once the waterworks began unexpectedly, they walked with us on and off throughout the day, helping us release the deep layers of grief which had collected and built up over time.

But do we have a "spirit of grief?" I would say not. Do we still grieve? That would be an emphatic *yes*. Is it something you can get completely free from? It's hard to say. There will *always* be birthdays, anniversaries and the holidays each and every year, and it's impossible to know if a memory or a tender place will be prodded, sparking an emotional response. "But you know your son doesn't want you being sad, with him living in the most incredible Place in all of creation!" Like we've mentioned before, he's there, we're here, and therein lies the dilemma!

The human heart was never designed to experience death or separation. God created us to only know abundant, eternal life with Him. Alas, sin came into the world, separated us from the Lord, and plunged us into an abbreviated, sub-standard Earth-life, dying and leaving those we love behind. It's a total rip-off for those left in the wake! Nonetheless, we eventually learn to carry on without them.

BEING STUCK IN GRIEF

We met a dear lady who seemed to be caught or stuck in her grief. She just kept asking how and why her loss could happen, and *many* years afterward she was still very paralyzed, which wasn't healthy for her or her family. At some point, one does have to reconcile with the loss and with God and put many of the questions to rest, at least until they are face-to-face with Him. As they begin to heal, eventually they must move forward for their own sake, as well as for their family and friends. But again the timing of that is between the Lord and the bereaved.

If you are a safe friend and you see your friend still stuck years later, then *maybe* the Lord would use you to help them. But please make sure the timing is right.

Hmm… I feel like we keep saying that, *and we do*—because it is so important!!

Understand this, my dear brothers and sisters: You must all be quick to listen, slow to speak. (James 1:19 NLT)

As we discussed previously, an often-said phrase by the well-meaning is, "It's been over a year; you really need to move on." But the more we loved, the harder we grieve, and the more time and grace we need to recover. The death of a close loved one changes you forever. The first year goes by like a blink—it's nothing in light of the long journey ahead of you, learning how to carry on with a gaping hole in your heart.

People think they know how to put us back together us once we "get broken." But most times, it adds much more stress and anxiety than help.

May *none* of us ever judge the grieving soul. Pray for them. Love them. Serve them. Comfort them. Be patient with them. But never judge them.

Until you've walked in their shoes, please don't judge, criticize or accuse.

SHOULD I SAY IT OR NOT?

Living on this side of Heaven, we will always walk through awkward situations.

I am always at odds now when it comes to wishing someone "Happy Mother's Day!" or "Happy Father's Day!" Should I say it or not? Are they even a parent? Maybe they've lost a child or had multiple miscarriages or not able to get pregnant. I know that will be a mindless gesture on my part to just "say it."

We were at a store on Father's Day, and the person helping us waited to wish Charlie a happy Father's Day until it was confirmed through our chatting that he has children. From one who has sustained loss, I see this as *very* thoughtful and considerate. Although we may be in the minority, we (bereaved parents) still do make up a decent segment of the populace! As well, there are those who may have just lost their beloved parent, so we must walk in sensitivity and not just assume.

During holiday services, a dear pastor friend of ours, after wishing a general greeting to everyone ("Merry Christmas!" or "Happy Mother's Day," and the like), *always* acknowledges those hurting on these "family holidays." The first time we attended a church service on one of these days, it meant *the world* to us to be affirmed like this! Even though it drew tears, our hearts were swollen with so much love and affirmation. (Thank you, Pastor Sean!) Generally, though, upon hearing these well wishes, although I am still so grateful to be a mother of two beautiful daughters living near us, it almost automatically happens that my thoughts go immediately to the one who is not with us anymore on this side. And *many* others experience this as well.

We can't just become dysfunctional and not say anything, but if you're with someone you know has sustained this type of tragedy, please try and remember to acknowledge their loss. It has been said to us by someone who knows, after tenderly wishing us a happy Mother's or Father's Day, "And I know Beau is sending special love to you from Heaven today." Just *some sort* of acknowledgment *means everything* at these times.

WHAT TO SAY

Many people long to know the right things to say to someone having recently suffered the death of a loved one. Here are few ways to approach this tender subject.

"How are you?" is the most standard and commonly asked question, especially to someone walking through a difficult time. Of course we absolutely know, you ask because you care. But please understand, in the case of loss, because you have to *know* they are "hurtin' for certain," each time someone asks this, it takes them right back to "that place" where it all started—the reason they are here in this moment.

Honestly, "How are you?" is not the optimal way to begin conversation with a griever. However if it's someone you are close with, you could modify the question to one like:

~ "How's it going? I can't imagine what you're walking through."

~ "How are you holding up? You've been on my heart constantly."

Or, rather than asking a question, instead, *tell* them something to show tenderness during this dark valley they are traversing, and don't be afraid to say the name of their beloved. A few examples are:

~ "I am *so sorry*. I can't believe _____ is gone! He/She was such an amazing person!"

~ "We have been praying for you and your family. We love you, and we/we'll really miss _____."

~ "There are no words to help, but please know we are so sorry and our hearts ache/break for you."

~ "I can't imagine all you are going through. We are just so sorry for all of your pain/heartache. It's got to be unbearable at times."

~ "I don't know what to say, but I love you. And you can talk to me about _____ whenever you like! I would be honored!"

~ "I've never walked this road so I can't relate fully to how you feel, but it's got to be so horrible. My prayers will certainly be with you in the coming weeks and months."

~ *"Please* let me know if you need *anything*. And if I don't hear from you soon, I'll be checking in on you!" (Then follow it up with action, because this offer often falls through the cracks! More to come about this.)

I think you get the drift.

Someone said so eloquently,

Each grief experience is unique. Responding to a griever should be unique too, sensitively based on the personal needs of the griever, and thoughtfully considering how to "best" respond to the situation.[42]

When speaking to someone who has tasted a different type of loss than my own, for example, loss by suicide or even murder, it's okay to add, *"I can't begin to comprehend what you're walking through. I have no words. I know what it's like to lose a child, but not what you have experienced."* These words can be like salve rather than sandpaper to the soul.

Talk to your friend about their deceased loved one! Not as if nothing ever happened, but with tenderness. Warmly say the name of the departed in conversation. We *love* to hear their name spoken.

IT IS NOW THE ELEPHANT IN THE ROOM!

Don't avoid the obvious. Your friend misses their special loved one more than you can imagine and *wants* to talk about them! Tell them how sorry you are, how much you miss him/her, how much he/she meant to you, how special they were. Tell a funny or touching story. (We got an *earful* of funny and "oh-my-gosh" stories from many of Beau's friends and cousins the week he left us. It meant *so much* to hear how he affected so many lives!)

A few years after Beau died, Jim and Lorraine lost their nineteen-year-old son who battled his entire life with birth defects that confined him to a bed or wheelchair. They asked us to sing at Jonathan's memorial service, since our music had been a continual source of life and peace in their home for years.

In working with the pastor of their church to discuss details of the service, Charlie mentioned about our own loss. Pastor Eric replied, *"Yes I'd heard about that. I'm so sorry. I knew Beau. I played bass with him and you guys back in 2005 when you ministered here in the valley."*

Whaaaaaat? And the tears (ours!) began to flow!

We began to discuss all about the journey. And just knowing he knew Beau and understood some of the depths of our loss gave us strength and affirmation, which brought a fresh wave of life and encouragement to our souls. And just hearing his name spoken again, especially from an unexpected source, was so extremely special and life-giving to us!

THEY WILL PROBABLY CRY. SAY IT ANYWAY.

Like in this example above, grieving people who recently lost someone so dear to them often *want* to talk about their departed loved one! Be warned—this will almost inevitably stir up tears; however, it's often a good thing! Although no one wants to be responsible for making someone else cry, these types of tears can be very therapeutic.

Crying is a place where they connect with their departed child, spouse, sibling, parent, or friend. "That place" is touched again, "that place" that came alive when their beloved died. Whenever someone mentions the loss, it usually will bring tears to the eyes, a lump in the throat, or cause their heart to swell with love, pride, and missing. But mostly, it brings tears—a few at least.

But that's okay! Believe it or not, we *want* to go there!! We *want* to talk about him or her! We *want* to recall how sweet or caring or funny or special they were to us and to so many! *Please* don't hold back talking about the one who died with those who loved them the most. The memory brings them a moment of closeness which breathes another breath of life into their soul.

We pray these tips and guidelines are helpful as you walk with your bereaved friend or relative, especially in the beginning days of their grief journey, but also into the months and years afterward as they recover and move forward.

CHAPTER FOURTEEN

Rules of Engagement

noun MILITARY specialized

Orders that soldiers fighting in a war are given about what they can and cannot do.

Cambridge Dictionary

We had a dear friend at church who raised twin boys on her own from the time they were very young. When they became ten years old, one of them developed a brain tumor, which ended up cutting his life extremely short, in spite of how fiercely she, the medical field, and the entire church fought to save his life.

In the months and years following, I was always so amazed at her beautiful smile any time I would see her before and after services, and not knowing better, would show my care by very sincerely asking how she was doing. I just couldn't believe how she seemed to just be "over it," after losing one of her young children!

But after we lost our own son, whom she knew well, we became suddenly so much closer, and she began opening up to me about her own grief journey. I learned her smile was a façade—a cover just so she could get through the crowds of people without showing her true feelings: the pain, the anguish, the confusion that she faced. For years she struggled with anger—at first with God, with the church, with the doctors, and with the bitter blow she had been dealt. Yet she carried on because she had another young life to pour into and raise. And in time, as with our own story, God eventually won her heart back by loving her back to Himself.

But to survive the onslaught of well-meaning individuals who continually reached out wanting to help but not knowing how (like me, sadly), she would cover her feelings and "put her best face forward" so they wouldn't probe and she could get through another day of survival. Only her loving Heavenly Father and very few individuals knew the deep grief she continued living with, long after her ten-year-old passed away.

Since you are reading this book, it shows *you care* about those hurting from a loss. Your desire is to see them recover, and you want to learn the best ways you can spare them any extra or unnecessary pain. We'd like to share a few general "ground rules" with you here, and we hope you will add these into your own toolbox of ways to help the hurting.

RULE 1: LOVE THEM

Love is a verb—an *action* word. *Show* them love in the form of patience. In the form of kindness. Of tenderness. Compassion. Care. As we mentioned before, offer to help with practical, specific items. Provide a meal you know they would like, or run an errand, mow the lawn, trim some bushes, plant some flowers, take their kids to rehearsal, pick up groceries. Observe their needs, and *look* for particular ways you can help.

Be proactive, because most grieving people won't ask. They just don't have the mental energy. Try to avoid saying, "Let me know if you need anything," because *chances are strong they will not ask*. But instead offer, "Let me come over and do the laundry," or "I'm going out; give me your grocery or hardware list." The neighbor of a newly widowed friend stepped up and cut their grass for an entire year after her husband passed away—a *very* thoughtful gesture.

Don't just assume, "She will definitely let me know if they need anything." Or, "So many people love these guys—I know someone else will step up and help." Number one, if there are a lot of people around in the beginning, just give it a little time. Once all the company goes home and life seems to be back to "normal" again, *this* is when a whole new level of grief and paralyzation will set in. This is a great time to step up and assist. Number two, so many people are offering to help, they won't remember who to ask if they do have an urgent need, and honestly may not be comfortable asking *anyone* for *anything*. So do be politely proactive, but if they are strongly insistent that they don't want anything, please don't push this issue.

If you have resources, give them some money for a dinner out, or restaurant/delivery service gift cards. One dear saint paid for my hair service just before Beau's memorial service. What a generous act of love.

In some situations, the family lets it be known that they prefer to be left alone—they just need space for a while. We must honor this, and again not take offense. It is *not* about us, but it *is* about them. So again, in time, reach out in love to them and offer ways to possibly assist or support them in whatever way presents itself. This type of selfless kindness will store treasures in Heaven for you.

RULE 2: DON'T JUDGE

As we mentioned earlier, may *none* of us ever judge someone grieving, since we don't fully know their story.

You read earlier about our friend's husband died unexpectantly in their home one morning after returning from the gym. It was such a shocking and horrible loss. Except for her single adult son and elderly mother-in-law, she had no family in town. She was so distraught and was emotionally numb for months. Most of her friends (but thankfully not all) eventually became silent, and even her pastor and their church stopped reaching out to her—she was out of sight and out of mind.

As her husband was the main income provider, it wasn't long until many in her community judged her for not selling the house and anything of value. It drove her into deep despair. Not only had she *suddenly* lost the love of her life, which is paralyzing in and of itself, but now it seemed the whole town felt they knew the best way to manage her life after the loss. You just never know what secret torment is going on in the heart of the grieving.

Show support. If someone is crying over a loss, hold them and weep with them without judgment. Walk with them. Work with them. *"Comfort the feebleminded"* (1 Thessalonians 5:14 KJV). If *anyone* is feebleminded, it's a grieving soul.

RULE 3: ALLOW THE GRIEVER TO TALK WHEN THEY ARE READY

Everything is just so unpredictable for the bereaved person. They aren't comfortable talking about their pain with just anyone, even though the inquiring party may sincerely care. It's just very complex, especially in the beginning. At the moment you ask, they may be in turmoil on the inside but not want to talk about it.

Let *them* call the shots—when *they* want to "talk about it," tell you intimate details, begin discussing future plans. We must continually remind ourselves that it is *not* about us, and even though we want to help them so badly, we must step back and wait until *they* are ready.

Let me share a fictional scenario based on many similar encounters of our own.

Allen and Denise just lost their child. They finally go back to church and see many people they haven't seen since the funeral, maybe a few months afterward. So happy to see them back and because he cares, Tom catches them after service and asks, "Hey guys! How are you doing?"

They answer, "Oh, hey, Tom. We're fine, thanks," with a friendly smile, and then walk on.

So Tom thinks, They must be doing pretty well, or I'm sure they would've said something else. After all, they smiled and looked so good.

But what he doesn't understand is, he asked a very complicated question, and they just couldn't take the time, energy, or emotion to address the subject at the moment, so they avoided it the best way they could, trying to not be rude.

RULE 4: DON'T BE OFFENDED

Try not to be offended or affected if they don't return your text, email or phone call. Again, keep in mind, it's not about *you*. It's about *them*. *Each* communication from friends and family is a huge blessing, but sometimes like we've mentioned, they are too paralyzed to respond. However, it *means the world* to hear from you , and *please* be assured, sending a text or calling simply to love on them, not "asking" anything, is *extremely* valuable!! As we read about God earlier in Psalm 31:7, *"You have seen my troubles, and you care about the anguish of my soul"* (NLT). Let's be like the Lord and *show* we *care* for those in mourning without expecting anything in return from them. The Lord will repay you for your kindnesses.

Now this does not mean that person won't ever laugh or enjoy life again; however, you must realize they will never be the same. And that's okay. In most cases, loss makes us become better people because we now understand this kind of pain and can be a help to so many others who are hurting, and be their "Jesus with skin on."

RULE 5: GIVE THEM SPACE IN THEIR HEALING JOURNEY

An untimely death or life-altering hardship changes a person. Forever. Some sustain the damage in a healthier way than others, but we must be there for them, regardless.

In our journey, along the way we would hear through the grapevine some people were saying, "We want the old Charlie and Jill back. They're really different and now they're always so serious." News flash—the old Charlie and Jill are gone and not coming back. A part of us died when our son died. But we believe a different but better version of us now exists, full of more compassion, more mercy, and even more faith than before.

One older gentleman told us that a part of him died when his adult child disowned him—it was like a death, so in one way we shared the same pain. Life can be so harsh.

A bereaved person has been stripped of their loved one, and is completely crushed on the inside. And like a crushed bone, it takes a L-O-N-G time to heal.

Our friends Helene and Ernie lost their grandson in a murder in 2019. Afterward, Ernie found and posted this eloquent quote:

> Grief is learning how to live with someone in your heart instead of in your arms.[43]

Some would say, "Oh, how beautiful," which it is, especially to the hearer who hasn't walked through it. To those of us who have, we would call it more like brutal reality. *And* beautiful.

RULE 6: REMEMBER WITH THEM

Regarding the loss of a child or any close loved one, it means *so much* to the parent and the family to hear from others on the their birthdays, holidays, anniversaries, and the like. We encourage you to email, call, or text the parent or loved one when you have a memory about them. One of Beau's high school friends recently wrote us on the anniversary of his death, telling a beautiful story of how her life was forever impacted by how kind and thoughtfully he treated her at school, even as an underclassman! The tears surely streamed down our cheeks once again!

Some have created ways to honor or memorialize a lost one: planting a tree, a balloon or luminary release, planning a special meal honoring the person, donate to a mission or cause in their name, create a scrapbook or art project, purchase a memorial park bench if available. In the St Louis Zoo is a bronze drinking fountain donated by some friends of ours whose young son died in his sleep. It is a lasting memorial to his abbreviated life, even decades later. One author said,

> Parental grief does not "go away" or "get better," it just changes over time. Remember the above and you will become a positive part of a parent's grief journey, and not an invalidating memory during the worst time in their life.

And may we also add, this goes not only for bereaved parents, but for any heart-wrenching loss.

RULE 7: DON'T TRY TO "FIX" THEM

We know a couple who put on retreats for grievers, instilling hope into them that they can carry on. What a powerful ministry they have at SparkOfLife.org! One of their video blog titles is, *No Fixing Allowed.*[44] Interesting! In this blog, our friend stresses the importance of allowing those struggling with grief, the *permission* to grieve when they need to. They *must* allow themselves this painful but precious gift, which will become a path to healing in their life.

We all want *so badly* to restore our broken friend or loved one, to help them get past their pain and get on with their lives, putting all this behind them. But just like the Lord had us share with a congregation whose pastors' son was tragically killed, "*You* do the *loving*, and *I* (the Father) will do the *fixing*," we must step back and trust, because *He* will fix them. In time.

In Psalm 139 we see how the Lord knows all the ins, outs and intricacies of how we are wired, and He knows how to restore the broken! When we try to shortcut the process, with best intentions of course, it often ends up in a botched repair job which will cost the bereaved in longer recovery time.

Our friend Jeff was in the service department at a car dealership and saw a large sign hung on the wall reading, "We are the Maker and the Repairer." What a great way to also describe our loving Father! He is our Maker and our Repairer, and He is able to heal our broken hearts and bind up our wounds!

In a nutshell, I think this scripture sums it all up,

…being confident of this very thing, that He who has begun a good work in you will complete it until the day of Jesus Christ. (Philippians 1:6)

As we walk beside our grieving friend, we must trust that our Father is doing His good work in their heart and soul. He is faithful and kind.

CHAPTER FIFTEEN

Fah-KLEMPT (adj.)

There is no way to predict how you will feel.
—Rabbi Earl Grollman

Have you ever heard this term? Having several Jewish friends who became Christians as teenagers during the Jesus Movement, some of the Yiddish terms they use have integrated into our own "slanguage" through the years. One of them is the word *fah-klempt*, which is how we all would say it. (Actual spelling: *verklempt*.) Another one is *schlokah*. And among others: *nosh, kozzerai, schlep, meshugenah, schmooze, fermished*, and *oy!* They've become such perfect ways to express ourselves sometimes!

One online dictionary defines *verklempt* this way:

Verklempt is a loan word from the Yiddish language that acts as an adjective. It means to be overwhelmed by emotion, perhaps so much that one cannot speak.

Alternative spellings include ferklempt, farklempt, verklemmt, and faklempt.[45]

In our circles, *faklempt* has morphed into describing a wide variety of people who are basically dysfunctional, for whatever reason.

We've found it's just such a great word to accurately describe some people, which carries with it a slight bit of endearment without sounding harsh or judgmental. "Dysfunctional" can come across somewhat critical, depending on the circumstances.

Why in the world, some may ask, would I talk about something like this in a grief book? Because of this: Grief makes a person dysfunctional (at least temporarily). But I would rather say *fah-klempt*.

We don't act like we used to. We don't think like we used to. Some of what used to be funny to us, isn't anymore. We may be more intolerant toward some things, or we may take more liberties than we used to before. We have less patience with things that used to not bother us. We have to work harder on being kind to people who don't understand loss and who say insensitive things about what we've been through.

If we had a black-and-white temperament before, we may be even more that way afterward. And for those who were more easygoing, have difficulties making decisions, or were phlegmatic in temperament, may become even more indifferent toward important things—not able to make good decisions, or even make decisions at all!

We become *fah-klempt*.

We may not be comfortable around a lot of people. Or, we may *only* be comfortable hiding in a large crowd. We may exercise poor judgment in choices we make and do things that none of our friends understand.

We find ourselves impaired and unable to function.

Grief is hard, and those who haven't walked this road don't really understand. They only observe the odd behavior of their friend or relative and are bewildered by their actions.

But, on the other hand, grief may cause us to be more compassionate toward a hardship someone is suffering. We may be more loving to our family because we appreciate them more, since we all suffered the same loss but on different levels. When someone else loses a loved one, we are quick to jump in and offer help, knowing what they're going through and offering an empathetic ear. We want to help the hurting more. We realize the brevity of life on a deeper level and begin to look at weighing our moments with more consideration, knowing each day is a gift.

Rabbi Grollman writes these poignant thoughts:

You are looking at this irrational world with different eyes.

Because you yourself have experienced grief, you are better able to understand the heartaches of others.

You are more aware than before of what is significant and what is trivial.

And he quotes Friedreich Nietzche by adding,

That which does not kill me makes me stronger.[46]

Grief certainly has caused *us* to become somewhat *fahklempt* in areas, and has made us more aware of some of our weaknesses. But it certainly has allowed us to rise up stronger and shine brighter in other areas!

…For when I am weak, then I am strong. (2 Corinthians 12:10)

CHAPTER SIXTEEN

What about Faith?

Now faith is the substance of things hoped for,
the evidence of things not seen.

—Hebrews 11:1

So, what about faith? That's a good question! And one that I (Charlie) have contemplated many times since we lost Beau. I'll tell you right up front that we do not have all the answers, but I've laid out some thoughts about this journey of faith that have helped me, and I hope will help you as well.

First of all, as I looked at the eleventh chapter of Hebrews, I saw the great heroes of faith and the amazing things these men and women did *by faith*. It is quite astounding to read and then discover how the chapter ends with testimonies of some who did not see the victory on this side. Yet the Bible tells us, *"These all died in faith, not having received the promises"* (Hebrews 11:13). Scripture continues:

Others were tortured, not accepting deliverance, that they might obtain a better resurrection. Still others had trials of mocking and scourging, yes, and of chains and imprisonment. They were stoned, they were sawn in two, were tempted, were slain with the sword. They wandered about in sheepskins and goatskins, being destitute, afflicted, tormented, of whom the world was not worthy. They wandered in deserts and mountains, in dens and caves of the Earth. **And all these, having obtained a good testimony through faith, did not receive the promise,** *God having provided something better for us, that they should not be made perfect apart from us.* (Hebrews 11:35–40)

These great men and women of God died in faith! They were willing to lay down their lives for the Lord knowing God had a better place for them. They did not receive what was promised in this life, but *by faith* but they saw God's deliverance. They saw in their hearts a time when Jesus would come and redeem mankind with His blood, making us righteous, holy, unblameable, and irreprovable in His sight. They knew their faith would not be complete apart from us and this great salvation.

Although this promise is specifically referring to the salvation purchased for us through Christ, it clearly shows us that faith, in some cases, is more than seeing an answer to a prayer, but staying strong in the face of pain, disappointments, and even death.

Yes, *"faith can move mountains,"* and *"all things are possible to them that believe!"*[47] But the Bible also shows us that some received their miracle on this side of Heaven, and some didn't, but they *all* died in faith. It takes great faith to suffer through a painful or debilitating illness and keep your heart and mind on Jesus. It takes great faith to face death and continue to praise your God. That's the other side of faith— standing in the face of difficulties and trusting the Lord, no matter the outcome.

It reminds me of Shadrach, Meshach, and Abednego when they answered the threats of King Nebuchadnezzar:

If we are thrown into the blazing furnace, the God whom we serve is able to save us. He will rescue us from your power, Your Majesty. But even if He doesn't, we want to make it clear to you, Your Majesty, that we will never serve your gods or worship the gold statue you have set up. (Daniel 3:17–18 NLT)

Wow! That is some *bold* faith!

And notice Habakkuk's declaration, commonly called "A Hymn of Faith" (which inspired my song by the same title):

Though the fig tree may not blossom,

Nor fruit be on the vines;

Though the labor of the olive may fail,

And the fields yield no food;

Though the flock may be cut off from the fold,

And there be no herd in the stalls—

Yet I will rejoice in the Lord,

I will joy in the God of my salvation.

The Lord God is my strength;

He will make my feet like deer's feet,

And He will make me walk on my high hills. (Habakkuk 3:17–19)

Now this is amazing faith, and it's just like the faith of Paul—singing while in prison and encouraging us to rejoice in the Lord. Then we read about all the apostles who stood in faith throughout their persecuted lives and even as they faced their cruel deaths—they certainly died in faith!

The morning of Beau's death, Rick, a dear pastor friend, came to our home and said these poignant words, which we pondered for many months, and still do to this day: *"There's a faith to move mountains, and there's a faith to stand when the mountain doesn't move."*

He looked me in the eyes and said, "Charlie, that's where you are right now!"

God knows how I cried out for the kind of faith to stand through this nightmare. Like Jeremiah, I lamented, *"Everything I had ever hoped for is gone"* (Lamentations 3:17 NLT). But somehow I had to believe that even though everything in me was broken, God would help me.

I wanted to run, and much of me did run, but I'm *so* thankful to God that *He ran with me*. His love and grace surrounded me even when I didn't feel it or realize it. Yes, He was giving me faith to stand, and I *really* needed it, because our mountain of sickness and disease did not move.

In the natural we lost the most important battle of our lives. But, in light of Heaven and eternity, of course, we didn't lose. The scripture says, *"Death is swallowed up in victory"* (1 Corinthians 15:54). Yes, even when it looks like we lost, thank God we really did win; ultimately, our son made it to Heaven and is living in the fullness of awesomeness, *way* beyond our imagination!

Like one minister who lost his daughter said to me in closing his email, "Congratulations on getting one of your kids to Heaven!"

Even if you lose the fight of faith for your loved one on this side, please know that you have not lost the entire battle. The enemy cannot claim ultimate victory, because he lost *everything* at the cross, and all he has left are lies and accusations. Even though all *seems* lost, you have not lost the entire battle.

In time our hearts began to heal, our eyes, after being so blurred with tears, became more opened, and we could rejoice in this truth. And so will you.

So when this corruptible has put on incorruption, and this mortal has put on immortality, then shall be brought to pass the saying that is written: "Death is swallowed up in victory."

"O Death, where is your sting? O Hades, where is your victory?"

The sting of death is sin, and the strength of sin is the law. But thanks be to God, Who gives us the victory through our Lord Jesus Christ. (1 Corinthians 15:54–57)

Although we knew Beau had received the ultimate victory, it was still so difficult for us, living on this side of Eternity without him. We had to guard our hearts because we knew satan was trying to take us out just like he tried with Simon Peter. Jesus said, *"Simon, Simon! Indeed, satan has asked for you, that he may sift you as wheat. But I have prayed for you, that your faith should not fail."* (Luke 22:31–32)

Peter was one of Jesus' closest disciples with a huge call on his life, and satan had it out for him. Jesus knew it and prayed for him in advance that his faith would not fail. Thank God, Peter's faith did not fail in the end! Even after denying his Savior and Friend, weeping bitterly with shame (and I'm sure a lot of self-condemnation), he eventually was able to receive forgiveness from Jesus, and forgive himself as he moved forward into his powerful calling.

We are so grateful for our entire community of family, friends, and fellow ministers who kept us in prayer. I'm sure many were praying we would not lose our faith. Although it may have appeared we did for a time, thank God we did not (at least not for too long!). Yes, like Peter we wept bitterly and wavered. It was a difficult time of trying to reconcile everything that happened. But eventually, and completely by the grace of God, we got back on our feet. Jesus said,

"The blessing of Heaven comes upon those who never lose their faith in Me, no matter what happens." (Luke 7:23 TPT)

Speaking of not losing your faith no matter what, let's look closer at Paul's life of faith. Nothing would move this man, no matter what came against him:

I have worked much harder for God, taken more beatings, and been dragged to more prisons than they. I've been flogged excessively, multiple times, even to the point of death. Five times I've received thirty-nine lashes from the Jewish leaders. Three times I experienced being beaten with rods. Once they stoned me. Three times I've been shipwrecked; for an entire night and a day I was adrift in the open sea. In my difficult travels I've faced many dangerous situations: perilous rivers, robbers, foreigners, and even my own people. I've survived deadly peril in the city, in the wilderness, with storms at sea, and with spies posing as believers. I've toiled to the point of exhaustion and gone through many sleepless nights. I've frequently been deprived of food and water, left hungry and shivering out in the cold, lacking proper clothing. (2 Corinthians 11:23–27 TPT)

Wow. Just *wow!* I can hardly imagine how hard that would have been, but by the unceasing, empowering grace of God, he never lost his faith.

> *We are hard-pressed on every side, yet not crushed; we are perplexed, but not in despair; persecuted, but not forsaken; struck down, but not destroyed.* (2 Corinthians 4:8–9)

Paul's mountains were not moving, but thank God, he had faith to stand when the mountain didn't move. When he prayed three times for a thorn in the flesh to be removed, which was a messenger from satan, the Lord answered, *"My grace is sufficient for you, for My strength is made perfect in weakness."* (2 Corinthians 12:9)

Thankfully, He does give sufficient grace to help us in our time of need.

But some still ask, "Charlie, what happened? *How* could this happen? *What went wrong?"* I have chased a lot of questions, theories, opinions and rabbit trails to find answers to this, but they all seem to have holes in them. Our friend Andrew describes it this way: "Opinions are like noses, everybody has one, and they usually have a couple of holes in them." Well said!

Trust me, I have spent countless hours studying God's Word and praying about these questions, and I had determined from the start I would never let my experience determine my doctrine or my theology. Instead, I prayed that I would only let the Word of God dictate what I believe. So the more I studied, the more I began to see once again that Jesus is truly the Healer, and He is the same yesterday, today, and forever.

Honestly, it took *quite a while* to get back to this. For the first few years I could hardly read some of the Bible's "red letters" of Jesus' healing ministry, because it confused and frustrated me to see Him healing someone else's child and not mine. I hope you can understand this; I'm just being real here. But even though I still didn't fully understand exactly why my son didn't experience healing on this side of Heaven, I still saw clearly that Jesus was and always will be the Great Physician, He is the compassionate Healer, He *did* carry our sicknesses and diseases, *and* with His stripes we are healed. (1 Peter 2:24)

So, I finally made a choice to live in what I did know and not in what I didn't. I had to give the questions a rest and trust that someday I will understand, even if it means in Heaven. This is really the best and healthiest way to move forward in life, especially after a devastating loss.

Too often we waste precious time trying to figure out everything that happened instead of moving forward with what we do know—things I knew, like:

~ God is love, and nothing can separate us from His love.

Can anything ever separate us from Christ's love? Does it mean he no longer loves us if we have trouble or calamity, or are persecuted, or hungry, or destitute, or in danger, or threatened with death? (Romans 8:35 NLT)

~ He is the Father of Mercies and the God of All
Comfort.

*All praise to God, the Father of our Lord Jesus Christ.
God is our merciful Father and the source of all comfort.*
(2 Corinthians 1:3 NLT)

~ He heals the brokenhearted and binds up our
wounds.

He heals the brokenhearted and bandages their wounds.
(Psalm 147:3 NLT)

~ He collects our tears in His bottle and they are
precious to Him.

*You've kept track of my every toss and turn through the
sleepless nights, Each tear entered in your ledger, each
ache written in your book.* (Psalm 56:8 MSG)

These simple truths and so many more helped me run *to*
Him instead of away from Him. After all, like Peter said, *"Lord,
to whom would we go? You have the words that give eternal
life."* (John 6:68)

Let's not get all tangled up in the questions, doctrines,
controversies, and so on. These can rob you of life and peace.
At the same time, however, we must continue growing and
learning more of Him.

Bottom line is, we just don't see it all right now!

Now we see as through a glass, dimly, but then, face-to-face. Now I know in part, but then I shall know, even as I also am known. (1 Corinthians 13:12 MEV)

Let's also look in another translation:

Now we see things imperfectly, like puzzling reflections in a mirror, but then we will see everything with perfect clarity. All that I know now is partial and incomplete, but then I will know everything completely, just as God now knows me completely. (NLT)

There will always be some things that are a little bit fuzzy on this side of Heaven. Especially when it comes to someone's death, it can be very complicated. There may be things which have happened in their life that no one else is aware of, which *can be* key factors as to why someone left this life too soon, but really, *only God knows*, and we shouldn't speculate.

The secret things belong to the Lord our God, but those things which are revealed belong to us and to our children forever. (Deuteronomy 29:29)

I urge you to avoid going on a witch hunt, trying to figure out why someone didn't get healed and even questioning their faith. So often we feel we have to know everything, when it really is not our business—it's between God and that person. So let's not get caught up judging—it's just not a healthy place. It doesn't do any good to come up with ideas of what and why this happened, since many times it just fosters gossip.

I realize we are simply trying to reconcile the *why*, since we know God's promises are true, and He is the Healer. I get that. But we must be careful to not judge someone else's journey, like Job's friends did. Instead, let's focus on helping the ones left behind and leave those questions for when we get to Heaven.

So if you have lost a loved one, please don't let the questions paralyze you and destroy your future. We can't let our past take us out—past disappointments, past failures or misunderstandings, things that didn't go right. We have to move forward, casting all our cares on Him (1 Peter 5:7), not leaning on our own understanding (Proverbs 3:5), leaving the past behind, pressing on to the things that are before us, and pursuing the goal to win the prize of God calling us Heavenward in Christ Jesus (Philippians 3:13)! That's a lot, but it's *all good!*

This does not mean *in any way* that we are leaving our loved ones behind—in fact we are moving toward them. They are in Heaven waiting for us, and we're getting one step closer to seeing them every day! And oh, what a glorious day that will be!!

We have determined to move forward in our lives and pursue God, whether we ever understand everything or not, and we pray you do the same. This is greater faith than knowing and understanding everything perfectly in this life. Jesus said, *"Blessed are those who have not seen and yet have believed."* (John 20:29)

I'll choose to believe when my prayers seem unanswered

I'll choose to believe when lies look like the truth

I'll choose to believe when the mountain doesn't move

In spite of the pain, O Lord, I'll believe the best of You.[48]

—"Choose To Believe" by Jill LeBlanc,
from the album *Your Love Remains*

I can see light in the midst of darkness

I can see hope in the face of death

I can see all these things 'cause my Father says it's so

I'm seeing by faith, I'm trusting the Lord.[49]

—"Seeing By Faith" by Charlie LeBlanc,
from the album *Keep Pressing On*

IN CLOSING

Thank you so much for daring to open these pages, whether it was out of need, desperation, obligation, desire, or just plain curiosity! We pray you have been helped and enlarged in your soul, either in getting through your own loss, or being better equipped in assisting someone else get through theirs.

A RECAP

To our bereaved friend, although our paths may have never crossed, as you read this, we want you to know we love you, pray for you and we understand some of this type of pain.

If you have experienced the untimely, unexpected death of a close loved one, as difficult as it is early on, you must know that somehow you will make it through this dark and gut-wrenching time.

Do not compare yourself with anyone else who is grieving—your grief journey is unique to you.

Be patient with yourself and others; well-meaning people will say things that don't help. Just bear with them.

There may be times you feel paralyzed in your mind—you are not losing it!! This is completely normal and will eventually subside. In the meantime, find safe people you are comfortable sharing your pain with, knowing they will not judge or try to "fix" you.

Above all, be kind to yourself. Don't push yourself into doing things that don't have to be done *now*. Don't think about tomorrow—only focus on this moment of this day.

We pray you will find yourself in God's loving arms and grace. He alone is the Healer of broken hearts and the God of compassion. Jesus wept, He weeps with you, and He will help you.

My flesh and my heart may fail,

but God is the strength of my heart.

(Psalm 73:26 NIV)

To those walking beside the hurting, we want to encourage you to be that safe friend—that "Jesus with skin on," patiently listening without judgment.

The lyrics to an old song wisely encourage us,

Walk a mile in my shoes, Walk a mile in my shoes

Hey, before you abuse, criticize and accuse

Walk a mile in my shoes.[50]

Doing this, even just taking on this mindset, will change your outlook toward the sufferings of others, for sure!

The word God gave to Charlie that October day in 2010, *You do the lovin', and I'll do the fixin'*, was a message straight from Heaven to help us learn how to be a better channel of God's love to those who are suffering from loss. Don't try to fix them; just focus on loving them.

Before you speak, pray. Observe your friend's emotional state. Don't judge, don't try to "fix" them, but ask the Father how you should respond. What can you *do*—what does "love" look like at this moment in time? Pose the question in your heart, WWJD? (Truly, What Would Jesus Do?)

Since our Lord is the Father of mercies and the God of all comfort, may we always be His extended arms, hands, and mouthpiece in these difficult seasons of people's lives.

We must embrace the fact that it's not about us or even what we have to say, but completely about the one whose world has just fallen apart.

Our earnest prayer is that you would learn how to operate not only in sympathy toward the hurting, but also allowing compassion to flow from your heart, remembering what it was like when *you* have endured hardship, and what helped you during that time.

Rabbi Grollman states:

"Because you yourself have experienced grief, you are better able to understand the heartaches of others."[51]

And as we saw earlier, this goes right along with 2 Corinthians 1:4:

"He comforts us in all our troubles so that we can comfort others …[with] the same comfort God has given us." (NLT)

In the course of writing these pages over the past few years, several dear friends have passed on to be with the Lord, unfortunately, through awful maladies birthed by the enemy. We paused everything many times to go and "just be there" with the family of the deceased, as they walked through terrible grief following losing their loved ones. Seeing the value in our efforts, these moments made us even more determined to help as many as we can through sharing our thoughts.

We know there is still a lot we don't know, but we *do* know a few things. And we hope what we have shared will help you today and in the days to come.

When loss comes close to home, open your heart wide and allow the Lord's mercy and compassion to flow through you. You will make a lasting difference in others' lives, and become a better minister to those in need.

Finally and most importantly, to the one who has lost, please trust us in this:

You will make it, with God's help.

With sincere love and compassion,

Charlie and Jill

NOTES

1. Charlie LeBlanc, "You Never Leave Me," from the album *Your Love Remains,* © 2014 Joyful Word Music (Admin. by Joyful Word Ministries) / ASCAP / CCLI #7011183.

2. Merriam-Webster.com, s.v. "bereaved," accessed August 15, 2022, https://www.merriam-webster.com/dictionary/bereaved.

3. Phil Keaggy, "What A Day," from the album *What A Day,* ©1972 Browning Music/ASCAP.

4. Jill LeBlanc, "Worship You Forever" from the album *Simply Worship,* ©2012 Joyful Word Music (Admin. by Joyful Word Ministries) /ASCAP /CCLI # 6363750.

5. Jill LeBlanc, "Light of Heaven," from the album *Your Love Remains,* ©2014 Joyful Word Music (Admin. by Joyful Word Ministries) / ASCAP / CCLI #7011192.

6. Rabbi Earl A. Grollman, *Living When a Loved One Has Died* (Boston: Beacon Press, 1977; 1995), 15, 17.

7. Elisabeth Kübler Ross, *On Death and Dying* (New York: Touchstone, 1974; 1997).

8. Stephanie A. Sarkis, PhD, "Rebuilding after a Gaslighting or Narcisistic Relationship," July 12, 2019, *Psychology Today,* https://www.psychol ogytoday.com/us/blog/here-there-and-everywhere/201907/rebuilding -after-gaslighting-or-narcissistic-relationship.

9. Jill LeBlanc, "So Thankful," from the album *Your Love Remains,* ©2014 Joyful Word Music (Admin. by Joyful Word Ministries) / ASCAP / CCLI #7011196.

10. Grollman, *Living When a Loved One Has Died,* 23.

11. Ibid., 22–23.

12. Charlie LeBlanc and Jill LeBlanc, "God of All Comfort," from the album *Your Love Remains*, © 2014 Joyful Word Music (Admin. by Joyful Word Ministries) / ASCAP / CCLI #7011197.

13. *The American Heritage Dictionary of the English Language*, 5th ed., s.v. "grief," https://www.wordnik.com/words/grief.

14. *The Century Dictionary*, s.v. "grieve," https://www.wordnik.com/words /grieve.

15. Merriam-Webster.com, s.v. "grieve," https://www.merriam-webster.com /dictionary/grieve.

16. Grollman, *Living When A Loved One Has Died*, 14.

17. Dr. Colin Murray Parkes, *Bereavement: Studies of Grief in Adult Life*, Third Edition (International Universities Press, Inc. 1998), 6.

18. Earl A. Grollman, *Straight Talk about Death for Teenagers: How to Cope with Losing Someone You Love* (Boston, Beacon Press, 2014), 6.

19. "Bible Verses About Grief," Biblestudytools.com, accessed August 13, 2022, https://www.biblestudytools.com/topical-verses/bible-verses-for -overcoming-grief/.

20. Charlie LeBlanc, "Your Love Remains," from the album *Your Love Remains*, © 2014 Joyful Word Music (Admin. by Joyful Word Ministries) / ASCAP / CCLI #7011183.

21. Tony Cooke, "It's Okay to Cry," Rhema.org, accessed August 14, 2022, https://www.rhema.org/index.php?option=com_content&view=article &id=1071:its-okay-to-cry&catid=136&Itemid=304. Used by permission.

22. "Washington Irving Quotes," www.goodreads.com/quotes/44057 -there-is-a-sacredness-in-tears-they-are-not-a.

23. *Thayer's Greek Lexicon,* s.v. "sumpatheó," Strong's NT 4834, Biblehub .com, https://biblehub.com/greek/4834.htm.

24. Grollman, *Living When A Loved One Has Died*, 14.

25. "Smile," music by Charles Chaplin, lyrics by John Turner and Geoffrey Parsons, ©Copyright 1954 by Bourne Co. Copyright Renewed: All Rights Reserved International Copyright Secured.

26. Kelly Polley Giesler, "Speak Their Name," 2013, https://www.facebook .com/watch/?v=237226407098180.

27. T. J. Wray, *Surviving the Death of a Sibling* (New York: Three Rivers Press, 2003), 2, 4.

28. Ibid., 77.

29. Pastor Rick Warren, "How We're Getting Through," Saddleback Church, July 27, 2013, https://saddleback.com/watch/how-to-get -through-what-youre-going-through/how-were-getting-through ?autoplay=true, starting at the 5:08 mark.

30. "Jesus With Skin On," author unknown. Posted online at Mennonite World Conference, https://mwc-cmm.org/id/node/357.

31. Harriet Sarnoff Schiff, author of *The Bereaved Parent.*

32. Grollman, *Living When A Loved One Has Died,* 68, 69, 70.

33. Nora McInerny, "We don't 'move on' from grief. We move forward with it," TEDWomen 2018, https://www.ted.com/talks/nora_mcinerny_we_ don_t_move_on_from_grief_we_move_forward_with_it?language=en. Used by permission.

34. C. S. Lewis, *A Grief Observed* (New York: HarperCollins, 1961; 1996), 52, 53.

35. Sandy Fox, "Divorce Rate among the Bereaved," Open to Hope, August 4, 2009, https://www.opentohope.com/divorce-rate-among -bereaved/, https://ezinearticles.com/?Death-of-a-Child---Does-Loss-of -a-Child-Really-Destroy-Marriages?&id=5923085.

36. This quote is often attributed to Theodore Roosevelt, but no known source can be found to verify the attribution. https://www .theodorerooseveltcenter.org/Learn-About-TR/TR-Quotes?page= 112#:~:text=TR%20explained%20this%20in%20his%20book%2C%20 The%20Strenuous,know%20until%20they%20know%20how%20 much%20you%20care.

37. Angela Miller, quoted in ABedForMyHeart.com, walkwithme-nonprofit .org/quotes.

38. Grollman, *Living When A Loved One Has Died,* 12.

39. Litsa Williams, "I'm Grieving and You Don't Know 'Just How I Feel'" (blog), What's Your Grief?, June 5, 2020, https://whatsyourgrief.com /empathy-in-grief/.

40. T. J. Wray, Surviving the Death of a Sibling (New York: Three Rivers Press, 2003), 74.

41. Grollman, Living When A Loved One Has Died, 10.

42. Carol Ricks Bowman, "What to Say to Someone Who is Grieving," Grief&Loss, 2016, https://mygriefandloss.org/what-to-say-to-someone -grieving.

43. Lynda Cheldelin Fell, LyndaFell.com, Used by permission.

44. SparkOfLife, No Fixing Allowed, https://www.youtube.com/ watch?v=PcQ1zRww5QY.

45. grammarist.com, s.v. "verklempt," accessed August 15, 2022, https:// grammarist.com/spelling/verklempt/.

46. Grollman, Living When a Loved One Has Died, 110, 104, 111.

47. Mark 11:22–24; Mark 9:23.

48. Jill LeBlanc, "Choose to Believe," from the album Your Love Remains, © 2014 Joyful Word Music (Admin. by Joyful Word Ministries)/ASCAP /CCLI #7011190.

49. Charlie LeBlanc, "Seeing By Faith," from the album Keep Pressing On, ©1979 Joyful Word Music/ASCAP/CCLI #2017110/.

50. Joe South, "Walk a Mile in My Shoes," from the album Don't It Make You Want to Go Home, 1970, Capitol Records.

51. Grollman, Living When a Loved One Has Died, 104.

RESOURCES FOR GRIEF HELP

www.CharlieandJill.com/grief-help

A collection of blogs, stories, videos, and audio teachings to bring encouragement and affirmation.

BOOKS AND BLOGS THAT HELPED US

After our son passed away, we were groping for help, for comfort, for reconciliation. And we read *a lot!* Here are some of the blog sites and books we read that challenged, enlightened, and brought us hope. Although we don't necessarily embrace each theological point expressed, still we came away with rich, sustaining hope and encouragement that helped us to keep pressing on. Maybe you'll find some help here too.

Websites

~ WhatsYourGrief.com

~ SparkofLife.org

~ ABedForMyHeart.com

~ GriefShare.org

~ InternationalGriefInstitute.com

Books

~ *Living When a Loved One Has Died*, Rabbi Earl Grollman

~ *Imagine Heaven*, John Burke

~ *Surviving the Death of a Sibling*, T.J. Wray

~ *The Bereaved Parent*, Harriet Schiff

~ *Bereavement: Studies of Grief in Adult Life*, Colin Murray Parkes

~ *My Companion Through Grief*, Gary Kinnaman

~ *Life after Death*, Tony Cooke

~ *Within Heaven's Gates*, Rebecca Springer

~ *A Grief Observed*, C.S. Lewis

WE HAVE A FREE GIFT FOR YOU:

An album download full of songs to comfort you.

We have compiled a collection of songs to bask in God's beautiful love, find a healing balm for your broken heart, and infuse hope into your wounded soul.

Scan the QR code below with the camera app on your device.

Fill in your contact info.

You will then receive an email with the instructions to download the album to your device.

Time and space do not allow us to mention each person whose priceless love, prayers, and encouragement kept us moving forward during the fight and during the recovery. However, we must mention a few in particular whose contributions were particularly impacting.

VERY SPECIAL THANKS TO:

To all those who knew, loved and miss our son, Beau—what a tremendous loss we have all sustained. Thank you for your love, prayers and encouragement to and for our family as we have navigated this unwanted "new normal." Your support has meant the world to us and has been a major part of our healing journey.

Andrew and Jamie Wommack: For all of your generosity, love, and patience during *our* healing journey, giving us so many opportunities to minister and lead worship even when we were still so wounded. We will be forever grateful.

Dave and Joyce Meyer: Your generosity and support through the battle and after was a lifeline for us, including covering the cost of a private flight to move us from Arizona to Florida to continue Beau's treatment. Your kindness will never be forgotten.

Butch and Julieann Hartman: You have been some of our biggest cheerleaders, helping us birth this baby! Your in-our-face "motivational talks" (ha!) are what we needed to stay on task and finally cross this finish line! :)

Stephen Bransford: "Leading by example" in your own writing and taking your time to mentor and help guide us helped make this book be what it is today. Without your involvement and encouragement, it would've turned out a much different project.

Pat and Sue Bradley: Having released your own first book a year ahead of ours (and what a *great* book!), sharing advice with us and things you learned along the way was a huge impetus for helping us through much of the process, not to mention *all* your support, love, and encouragement through the years. You two are so special to us!

Wayne Hastings: We appreciate your patience with us, having come to you at Pat's suggestion, *so green* in the world of book writing! Thank you for your many enlightening advisory sessions full of guidance, words of wisdom, and for connecting us with Jenn.

Jennifer McNeil: What a privilege to have a highly experienced, professional editor who was not only excellent but very kind, patient, and flexible. It was a delight working with you!

Brad Herman and the Harrison House team: Our first conversation, doused with passion and tears, sealed the deal for me. Your hearts for this book made all the difference!

Steve and Lorrie Cain: What kind and generous souls! The level of encouragement, prayer, and support you have been to us in these projects the last few years, including this one, has been a refreshing breeze to us many times!

Jeff and Patsy Perry and SLFC: You guys are wired to jump into someone's crisis! Can't thank you enough for all of your prayer support while we fought together to save Beau, as well as after his departure. Thank you so much for hosting our Missouri memorial for Beau and the wonderful reception following. Then to top it with the financial support you gave— you all were just a massive help to us.

Phil and Lori LeBlanc: Where do we begin with you two? You and your family took Beau under your wings as one of your own when he moved to Phoenix for school. Following his diagnosis and beginning of treatment, the way you completely opened your home to our family was beyond generous. After he left us, you, Melissa, and our Phx Family put on that beautiful reception after the Arizona memorial service. Then you allowed us to use your beach condo to hide away for almost four weeks, which was such an incredible gift that allowed us to begin catching our breath. After that, your help was invaluable with tying up all his "loose ends" (selling his car, closing his bank account, etc.), and not to mention the countless times praying for us, crying with us, and just being there for us. "Thank you" seems so insufficient. Forever grateful.

Jennifer Kutscher: my sister, friend, and fellow comrade in the fight for Beau's life (along with countless others!). You lived with us and served as our administrative assistant during those years, and I can't imagine how we would've done this without you. We were away from home for eight months *during* the fight for Beau's life, with only a couple of short visits to see Mom and Dad (and *you*), and then several more months *afterward* with our recovery and travels. You took care of our home, the cat, and the dog like they were your own, along with keeping the ministry office open and functioning. What a Godsend to have you beside us, Jenne, especially during that time. We love you so much!

Kimette "Nurse Kim" and Rusty Maple: There are just too many to recount, all the ways you supported us in the last month of Beau's life—from cooking to errands, taking the midnight shift in staying up with me, to the endless ways you served us, to your financial support, and even getting our memorial tattoos together afterward! Now, knowing that our sons are together in Heaven, to think that you have had to endure the same horror when your precious Jesse left us just ten years later is unfathomable. Our hearts are forever joined!

Tom and Suzanne Ewing and Scott and Val Connor for making their two unoccupied condos in Scottsdale available to us for the two months we were driving to the Mayo every day. Your extreme generosity gave us the space we needed to dive into this operation of working to get our son well without spending unthinkable amounts of money on rentals, or burning out family members we would have stayed with during those seven weeks in Phoenix. Words are extremely insufficient to express the depths of our gratitude. And Tom and Suzanne, even though we ruined the surface on one of your coffee tables with Beau's leaky humidifier, you so kindly shared how you saw it as a memento, a reminder of how honored you were to have been a part of Beau's journey (sniff, sniff). I'm sure you don't still have that table after all these years, but your kindness and compassion shown will *never* leave our hearts.

Doug Fowler: We will never forget your generosity in opening up your home and supporting us all during the fight for Beau's life during those five months working with the Mayo in Jacksonville. Although it was a major invasion on your life and family, we will always remember your hospitality with extreme appreciation and gratitude.

Sally Stepanek Cox: A *major* player in getting us moving on this project, helping us realize that *we can do it*, and promising to be our editor to bring it to fruition—a *huge* answer to prayer for us, which fueled our hope of this actually becoming a reality! Tragically Sally's life was cut *way too short* through illness, but her legacy lives on in these pages!

Tony and Lisa Cooke: For taking the time early on to sit with us, encourage us, and weep with us!

John and Susan Donnelly: Our very dear Scottish friends who stood by us and stood up for us as we walked through those terribly painful and paralyzing early days!

Gary Kinnaman: Our long-time friend, for writing your compassionate book on grief and introducing us to Rabbi Earl Grollman through those pages.

Mark and Kristina Buckley: For meeting with us in those early, very raw days shortly after our loss, and reopening the wounds of your own loss so you could share and help us.

The many wonderful friends who shared their homes with us as a place to get away and work on writing:

~ John and Alisa Williamson, Sturgis, SD

~ Teri Secrest, South Ponte Vedra Beach, FL

~ Jake and Mary Beckel, Marshall, NC

~ Butch and Julieann Hartman, Los Angeles, CA

In remembrance of our dear friends and family who left this life too soon, near the time or after our son did, until this printing.

Haylie Grace Willard, 2004

Zachary Brady, 2005

Beau Charles LeBlanc, 2009

Becky Hoeft, 2009

Nancy Demus, 2010

Levi Patrick, 2010

Katie Cavanaugh, 2010

Micah Bauer, 2010

Kelly Coulter, 2010

Delaney Gralike, 2013

Chase Lovelace, 2013

Christian Shea Kennet, 2014

Bubble Richardson, 2014

Jonathan Berry, 2014

Linda Perry, 2015

Dana Edmonds, 2015

Dave Duell, 2015

John David Wiese, 2016

Bob Ward, 2016

Glenna Dyer, 2016

Jimmy Pinzensham, 2017

Jonathan Bachert, 2017

Mike McKinnis, 2018

Jesse Maple, 2018

Kay Keller Serven, 2018

Chris Bergman, RFJ, 2018

Megin Ward, 2018

Sally Stepanek Cox, 2019

Todd Radke, 2019

Danny Maloney, 2020

Jordan Sky Pearson, 2020

Bodhi LeBlanc, 2020

Clifton Coulter, 2021

Rich Riehl, 2022

Mark Abernethy, 2022

Jason Provinse, 2022

Evan Bransford, 2022

Reed Grafke, 2022

Rose Torrence, 2023

And so many others not listed here.

ABOUT CHARLIE AND JILL LEBLANC

Charlie and Jill LeBlanc have been serving the Lord together in music ministry and Bible teaching for over 40 years and are passionate about honoring the Lord, helping hurting people, and encouraging others through their music and ministry.

The LeBlancs place major emphasis on the Word of God in their songs, focusing on how wonderful our Heavenly Father is and all that Jesus accomplished for us in His death and resurrection. They lead praise and worship; speak and sing in churches, Bible schools, seminars, and conferences; as well as mentor and train other worship leaders and music teams. They have served as conference worship leaders for Joyce Meyer Ministries and Andrew Wommack Ministries for several years, and Charlie led worship on two of Integrity's *Hosanna!* music releases. They are seasoned singer/songwriters with over 100 songs recorded on more than 20 albums distributed worldwide including their best sellers, *My Strength My Song, Your Love Remains, Simply Worship,* and *Redeeming Blood.* Their travels have taken them to over 25 nations in almost every continent.

With the loss of their 23-year-old son in 2009 and the release of their first book, *When Loss Comes Close to Home,* they have now entered a new season, watching God birth another whole avenue of ministry to the bereaved and the hurting, restoring hope and healing to wounded hearts.

They live in northeast Florida near their two daughters' families and are enjoying their four grandsons when they are home!

ABOUT OUR MINISTRY

www.CharlieandJill.com

Since 1980, after graduating from Rhema Bible Training Center in Tulsa, Oklahoma, Charlie and Jill have answered "The Call" to serve the Lord full time, doing their part in reaching the world with the love of Jesus.

Their website is a rich resource to help you in your Earth journey. You will find numerous teaching blogs, along with music albums filled with songs of encouragement, worship, faith, and comfort in the Lord.

Follow them on:

YouTube: Charlie and Jill LeBlanc

Facebook: Charlie and Jill LeBlanc

Instagram: @charlieandjill

Twitter: @charlieandjill_

Listen on all music streaming platforms such as Spotify, Apple Music, Pandora, Amazon Music.

You can stay connected with Charlie and Jill by subscribing to their email list and mailing list through their website, or contact their office by calling or writing:

Joyful Word Ministries

P.O. Box 2733

Ponte Vedra Beach, FL 32004 (USA)

Toll free in US: 1-800-326-0741

Website: www.CharlieandJill.com

Email: mail@charlieandjill.com

In the Right Hands, This Book Will Change Lives!

Most of the people who need this message will not be looking for this book. To change their lives, you need to **put a copy of this book in their hands.**

Our ministry is constantly seeking methods to find the people who need this anointed message to change their lives. **Will you help us reach these people?**

Extend this ministry by sowing 3 books, 5 books, 10 books, or more today, and become a life changer! Your generosity will be part of catalyzing the Great Awakening that many have been prophesying and praying for.

Your Love Remains

Songs of comfort, hope, love & trust. When everything else crumbles around you, His Love Remains above everything. Available in CD and Download

Joyful Word Ministries, P.O.Box 2733
Ponte Vedra Beach, FL 32004 USA
1-800-326-0741

Now Available in Digital Format!

Charlie and Jill's catalogue is now available on
two USB Flash Drives:
Six-Pack Plus
Timeless Collection
For more details, visit

www.CharlieandJill.com

or call 1-800-326-0741